Praise for *Spiritual Leadership*

"Eddie Hammett has done a superb job of d[...] the culture of most established Protestant congregations and the secular, postmodern, post-Christian culture that reflects the emerging young adult generation. Then he offers clear counsel as to how congregational leaders can negotiate the transition. Eddie draws on years of rich personal experience in dealing with these issues. He also offers a wealth of resources…books, videos, Web sites, etc. This is a wonderful manual for congregational leaders who are motivated to be changed and to lead change."

ED WHITE, The Alban Institute

"Hammett offers a wide variety of insights, tools, and resources to help any church to move from maintenance to mission in order to build bridges into the lives of those around them. This is a 'how-to' resource I can recommend to any church leader who desires to make an impact for Christ in this secular age."

GENE WILKES, author of *Jesus on Leadership*

"The title of my friend Edward Hammett's new book, *Spiritual Leadership in a Secular Age,* is a what-you-see-is-what-you-get essential for heads-up church leaders, both volunteer (lay) and vocational (staff). By writing as coach rather than consultant, Eddie enables leaders to execute his 'plays' for 'big wins.' His practical relevance, drawn from decades of personal struggle and learning, produces practicable designs for bridging the gap between leaders' practiced spirituality and a pervasive, and often perverted, secular culture."

MELVIN J. STEINBRON, Lay Pastors Ministry, Inc.

"This book is loaded. It is loaded with great information, great resources, and great insights. Having taught in seven seminaries, I would say that this is the kind of book that I want my students to interact with. It's also a great resource for pastors, church staffs, and leaders."

FRANK R. TILLAPAUGH, author of
Unleashing the Church and *Calling*

"*Spiritual Leadership in a Secular Age* forces church leaders to look into the mirror, take a personal assessment of the state of their local church, and update their methods of reaching the increasingly secular world around them with the gospel of Christ. Hammett reasons well that if a church is not willing to change in order to reach the postmodern world, then the doors of that church may someday close forever. When the mission of the church becomes maintenance, the decline has begun. Hammett provides coaching aids, assessment tools, and excellent resources to move churches and church leadership from maintenance to mission."

RANDY FRAZEE, Pantego Bible Church, Fort Worth, Texas

SPIRITUAL LEADERSHIP
in a Secular Age

Other Lake Hickory Resources

Operation Inasmuch
by David W. Crocker

Pursuing the Full Kingdom Potential of Your Congregation
by George W. Bullard

Seeds for the Future
Growing Organic Leaders for Living Churches
by Robert D. Dale

———————

Available at
www.lakehickoryresources.com

SPIRITUAL LEADERSHIP
in a Secular Age

Building Bridges Instead of Barriers

Edward H. Hammett

Lake Hickory RESOURCES
ST. LOUIS, MISSOURI

Scripture quotations marked KJV are from the *King James Version* of the Bible.

Scripture quotations marked (NIV) are taken from the HOLY BIBLE, NEW INTERNATIONAL VERSION®. NIV®. Copyright © 1973, 1978, 1984 by International Bible Society. Used by permission of Zondervan Publishing House. All rights reserved.

Scripture marked NASB is taken from the *NEW AMERICAN STANDARD BIBLE* ®, © Copyright The Lockman Foundation 1960, 1962, 1963, 1968, 1971, 1972, 1973, 1975, 1977, 1995. Used by permission.

GOD'S WORD® is a copyrighted work of *God's Word to the Nations*. Quotations are used by permission. Copyright 1995 by God's Word to the Nations. All rights reserved.

"Are We a Mission or Maintenance Congregation?" chart on page 33 is from Ronald Russell, *Can a Church Live Again?* (Macon, Ga.: Smyth & Helwys, 2004). Used by permission.

Cover and interior design: Elizabeth Wright

Visit the Lake Hickory Resources Web site
at www.lakehickoryresources.com

10 9 8 7 6 5 4 3 2 1   05 06 07 08 09

Library of Congress Cataloging-in-Publication Data

Hammett, Edward H.
  Spiritual leadership in a secular age : building bridges instead of barriers / Edward H. Hammett.
    p. cm.
  ISBN 13: 978-0-827234-61-9 (pbk. : alk. paper)
  ISBN 10: 0-827234-61-9
  1. Christian leadership. 2. Church renewal. 3. Leadership–Religious aspects–Christianity. I. Title.
BV652.1.H24 2005
253–dc22

Printed in the United States of America   2004030026

Contents

SECTION 1
Where We Are Now: Spiritual Leadership *in* the Church

SECTION 2
Where We Want to Be: Spiritual Leadership *through* the Church

Inspiration and Wisdom for
Twenty-first–Century Christian Leaders

You have chosen wisely in deciding to study and learn from a **Lake Hickory Resources** book. Lake Hickory Resources publishes for

- congregational leaders who desire to serve effectively
- Christian ministers who pursue excellence in service
- members of a congregation that desires to reach its full Kingdom potential
- denominational leaders who want to come alongside affiliated congregations in a servant leadership role

Lake Hickory Resources is an inspiration and wisdom sharing vehicle of Lake Hickory Learning Communities. LHLC is the web of relationships developing from the base of Hollifield Leadership Center [www.Hollifield.org] near Hickory, North Carolina. LHLC addresses emerging strategic issues of leadership development for congregations, denominations, and parachurch organizations.

The mission of **Lake Hickory Resources** is currently being expressed through two meaningful avenues. First, George Bullard, executive coach for Lake Hickory Learning Communities, also is senior editor for *Net Results* magazine [www.NetResults.org], a national, trans-denominational publication that appears monthly in either print or electronic form.

Second, **Lake Hickory Resources** publishes books in partnership with the Christian Board of Publication. Once this partnership is in full production it will produce eight to twelve new books each year.

We welcome your comments on these books, and we welcome your suggestions for new subject areas and authors we ought to consider.

James H. Royston, Executive Editor
George W. Bullard Jr., Senior Editor
SeniorEditor@LakeHickoryResources.org

Lake Hickory Learning Communities is a ministry of www.NorthCarolinaBaptists.org.

You Can't Build a Bridge by Starting in the Middle

"I'll Meet You Halfway."

These words are meant to convey a message of positive compromise and reconciliation. But these words are problematic in the church. Why?

There are no halfway measures in the body of Christ. Jesus always went the whole way. Jesus never met anyone halfway, and gave no halfway models or pats on the back for lukewarm faith. The Divine did not meet the human halfway. God went all the way to a manger in Bethlehem to meet us. Jesus went all the way to a cross to save us. The Spirit went all the way to the ends of the earth to sustain us. When Jesus "descended into hell," in the words of the Apostle's Creed, he showed us that there are no lengths to which he wouldn't go to connect heaven and hell and to build a bridge between the worst humans could come up with and the best heaven had to offer.

Trying to build a bridge from the middle is like anchoring in quicksand. You can only build a bridge by arching the ends. The literal meaning of the word *religious* is "firm binding" or "re-binding." The essence of religious faith for the Christian is the firm binding and re-binding of extremes: connecting the human and the Divine, integrating the new in the old, the saint and the sinner (in all of us), the blue (the color of eternity) and the red (the color of mortality), becoming local in a global way, showing the relevance of irrelevance, loving others (including your enemies) so that you can find yourself.

The tameness and sameness of the church's preferences is the mark of a middle-of-the-road mentality that is increasingly problematic in the culture as well as in the church. Hollywood has found that the only movies that achieve "blockbuster" status are those that bind tightly together four quadrants: young and old, men and women. The middle-of-the-road is home to only one thing: road kill. Among First World nations, the U.S. now has the smallest middle class as a percentage of total population, and the largest population of poor and rich. Our success at bridging the gap between the very rich and the very poor will write the history of the future.

In this superbly engineered book, Eddie Hammett shows the church the art and science of "building bridges instead of barriers." He begins by connecting the church "for us" to the church "for them." Learning to be a disciple of Jesus in the sanctuary of a church ("for us" Christianity) is like learning to swim in a lap pool. You don't really know how to swim until you swim in the oceans of life ("for them" Christianity).

Hammett reveals that this book was birthed when "an unchurched spiritual traveler friend" asked him, "Why do churches and church people work so hard building barriers to keep me out rather than bridges to let me in?" His answer to that question is the suspense and suspension of this book. Instead of spending so much time talking to ourselves—the church loves to talk to itself and to hear itself talk, or, as Walker Percy put it while explaining why he loved Bruce Springsteen so much, "he sings of us while singing to us"—Hammett shows how to bring the best of church culture into connecting conversations with "secular culture," postmodern culture, emerging culture, non-Western culture.

Where there's a rift or a river, the church spans the gap by building a bridge. But not by starting in the middle. Or, in Hammett's more resonant phrasings: by starting with a church "for them," Christians will discover the church "for us."

Leonard Sweet
Drew Theological School
George Fox University
www.preachingplus.com

Leading *in, through*, and *as* the Church

Let me say up front, I know that many of you will likely question my definitions of "spirituality" and "leadership" and my use of "secular age" as you read this book. I would ask that you be patient and try to think outside and even beyond the traditional boxes and definitions we typically encounter. This book is designed to seek answers to four basic questions:

1. What are the ingredients of effective spiritual leadership in an increasingly secular world?
2. How can a leader and a community of faith build bridges instead of barriers in an unchurched culture?
3. What are the leadership forms and functions needed in an effective church ministering in the twenty-first–century world?
4. How can a leader maintain the integrity of one's faith while building bridges with an unchurched world?

These questions have emerged through workshops, seminars, online forums, and conversations around my previous three books. Much of this book, as with my other writings, comes out of my personal ministry. I've been intentional over the last decade about building relationships with unchurched persons who are spiritually thirsty but just can't find their place in traditional church life. I continue to be amazed at how many spiritual travelers are out there. I'm still committed to the institutional church that trained me, nurtured me, and helped me find Christ. However, I am just as committed to helping those who can't find their way into that church to find their way from brokenness to wholeness and health, and from aimlessness and searching to an anchoring in a sustaining and meaningful faith. I'm very concerned that the institutional church find ways to build bridges instead of barriers to these fellow strugglers in the faith. I'm also committed to helping the institutional church prepare itself for an effective ministry after the present church culture generation dies out. (This is happening very rapidly in many congregations across North America.) How can we learn to exercise spiritual leadership *in* the church, *through* the church, and *as* the church in our twenty-first–century world?

As you read, consider the challenges you and your congregation face when it comes to:

- Keeping people older than 60, while still reaching people younger than 40
- Attracting and keeping those from the unchurched culture
- Finding resources and programs that are effective in speaking to the needs of the churched and the unchurched of multiple generations
- Building effective discipling relationships in a fast-paced world.

I write this book from a coach perspective rather than from that of a consultant. That is, I really come to pose some well-framed powerful questions around life and organizational issues that many are facing and struggling with during these days of rapid and deep change. I will share stories from my own journey, shifts I have made and am making in my ministry. I will also acknowledge from the very beginning that I am a fellow journeyman. I am still learning and open to the move of God in my life and the lives of those I encounter. Each major section includes some coaching questions. I will not give you all the answers—I don't have them. Your situation and circumstance and your callings and spiritual gifts are different than mine. My hope is that you will find questions and challenges that help you experience "deeper depths and higher heights" of the love of God and the mission of the church in our twenty-first–century world.

Last, I will repeatedly ask you to exercise your skills of spiritual discernment. What is God is saying to you and your congregation about finding and taking the next steps in your journey to ensure that the Great Commission and the Great Commandment are fulfilled in this and the next generation?

Edward Hammett
Hendersonville, NC
www.transformingsolutions.org
April 2005

Acknowledgments

Spiritual Leadership in a Secular Age summarizes some of my struggles and learnings over the last several decades as a result of my decision to learn to communicate the Good News in an increasingly secular and postmodern culture. My role as senior leadership and discipleship consultant and senior coach for the Baptist State Convention of North Carolina has anchored me in the church culture during these decades. I am deeply grateful for their encouragement, blessing, and support of my writing efforts.

Many of the challenges, rewards, and learnings in this journey have been because of a group of spiritual travelers that God has allowed me to encounter. They have blessed me as they have opened their hearts to–and shared their search for God with–me and one another. To these spiritual travelers I dedicate this book, for many of the learnings come from countless hours of dialogue with them as we have searched together for the Good News in a pained and rapidly changing world. Suzanne Shepherd, Connie Taylor, David Walley, Janette Starnes, Randy Pierce, and Chuck McGuire have become close and trusted friends through the years. Their journeys have influenced each other and me as we search for truth, wholeness, health, and healing. I treasure their friendship and value their commitment and search for God.

I am also deeply grateful to Russ White of the Christian Board of Publication and George Bullard of Lake Hickory Learning Communities, who believed in this work. I delight in being invited to be part of the inaugural offering of leadership books of the Lake Hickory Resources imprint series. Also, Trent Butler has been a faithful and challenging editor who has improved my writing and helped make this a useful book for many. For George Bullard's vision, leadership, and commitment to the future I will always be grateful and am blessed to be a team player in helping manage the present while we birth the new.

WHERE WE ARE NOW

Spiritual Leadership *in* the Church

1

Challenges of a New Culture

Leadership Challenges

"I'm working harder than I've ever worked before in my church, but as the community gets larger the church is getting smaller. Some newcomers visit our church but they never come back. We've got a good preacher, great music, and a beautiful building. Can you help me understand what's going on?"

"Those people moving into our community are not like us. They are Northerners who have invaded the South. They are not like us." (This could just as well be Easterners and Westerners.)

"Can a divorced person serve as deacon or church leader?"

"Should we involve single parents or unwed parents in our parent/child dedication service?"

"We've visited your churches, and all we've discovered is they don't like us and we don't like them."

Learning to live and function effectively in a new culture has its challenges. I moved from a metropolitan area to a mountain community about five years ago and experienced some of what many of our church leaders and churches are experiencing. I learned some lessons of living in a new land, a new culture, and a new community with a population of unfamiliar persons. I am learning:

- Natives to the area see things differently than those of us transplants who have moved into "their land."
- The pace of life is slower for most people in the mountains, except for those of us who are transplants.
- Often, especially in the winter, the fog settles in, and traffic slows or even stops for a while, so weather occasionally sabotages your morning meetings.
- Winter brings snow and ice. Transplants from the North keep moving, but the natives cancel schools and delay openings of businesses for a little snow.
- Such cultural traditions often upset the Northerners who think such decisions are ridiculous. They have lived in areas where they counted snow in feet rather than inches, and their life went on regardless.

One morning while driving down the mountain, I was privileged to watch the fog begin to lift amidst the beautiful sunrise, with the dew glistening, just as I was experiencing the feeling of urgency to make it to a meeting on time. It was an "aha moment" for me. It was as if God said, "When the blanket of fog lifts from our churches, they will see all the beauty underneath. They will see my creation, the beauty of the mission field I have planted them in for the purpose of service."

This book is designed to help you discover those aha moments and respond to them. In each chapter you will find coaching questions to help leaders begin to work with what often seems like overwhelming fog and often disturbing realties of a new culture. The coaching questions are designed to help you move from where you are to where God wants you to go. The coaching questions will also provide focus and intentional plans for forward movement and action.

The first section of this book is for helping us focus the morning sun on some of the confusions and frustrations felt by many churches and leaders in this rapidly changing culture. The quotes in the beginning of each chapter represent true-to-life comments I have encountered over the years while working with churches. It is my hope that as you continue to read, the fog will begin to lift in your mind as the Spirit brings new understandings, new ministries, and an awareness of new strategies and leadership strengths that will assist you in being an effective spiritual leader in a secular age.

A typical day in my consulting and coaching world includes pastors' or laypersons' calling me, almost in a panic, because cultural issues are now impacting their churches. The world has been changing for decades, and most churches have battened down the hatches. They have protected their turf, beliefs, and programs. Still, they have survived because the "church culture" (those raised in church over the last fifty years) was strong and faithful in attendance and giving. Now all of a sudden these "other people" are outnumbering "us" and are moving in our communities and challenging our status quo. Our faithful church culture is beginning to age out. Now what does the church do? How do leaders maintain the integrity of the Good News in an increasingly secular culture? How do leaders manage the present while effectively birthing the future? As a sign of hope, many churches and leaders *are* being effective in this secular culture.

Yes, many leaders and churches face these challenges with great courage, faith, and innovation. One such church is Mission Baptist Church in Locust, N.C. I've watched them for about fourteen years now. God has moved them from a quiet, declining rural congregation thirty miles outside metropolitan Charlotte, to a thriving congregation now creating a third worship service and contemplating a second track for Bible study and small groups. Fourteen years ago a remnant group of their leaders along with their pastor caught a vision of becoming a disciple-making church. They committed themselves to learning the lessons of their new culture and growing to see the beauty of their landscape rather than staying in the frightening fog that was keeping them in their plateaued state. When the fog started to lift on a few, the new was seen. The commitment level of staff and remnant leaders grew, and now the church is thriving and has become a teaching church for others. You can find their full story in *Can a Church Live Again?* by their pastor Ronald Russell.[1] The remainder of this chapter reviews some of the challenges they and many other church leaders face.

People Are Different

The Context Is Different

The major context change is the challenge of learning to find and experience the sacred in what many label as "secular." When I speak of a secular age, and postmodern spiritual travelers, I'm keenly aware that there are many who are spiritually minded and many who are serious about their spiritual journey who cannot find their place in most of the existing institutional churches. Such a reality serves to remind us that biblically it was never intended that there be a dichotomy between sacred and secular. God is God of all of life and Creator of all people. He is a God of Monday through Sunday, twenty-four hours a day. Somehow religion has gotten confined through the centuries to a building, a time frame during the week and around certain rituals, leaders, and traditions. Today God is making Himself known again in many places, through many types of people, engaged in many different rituals and traditions. This book is about affirming the journey and understanding and highlighting that the movement toward God is a journey. Many are at different places along the journey—but all on a serious spiritual journey are valued and need a safe place to explore, to network, and to experience life together along the way. Leadership therefore takes on a little different role as we often lead by example by pulling people forward through coaching questions and relationships rather than pushing them into a "box of set expectations, practices, or programs." Faith is experienced, confirmed, and celebrated in the context of community often gathered in what some would describe as "secular places" (i.e., coffee shops, bookstores, office break rooms, or restaurants). One of the clear challenges in this new culture is for leaders to learn of the diversity of journey out there and to learn to create safe places and relationships as seeds are planted, nurtured, and ultimately harvested.

Demographics Are Different

Ray Bakke, a leading missionologist and author, says it best when he explains, "the south is coming north, the east is coming west and on all 6 [populated] continents people are moving to the cities."[2] He further declares, "Mission—as it gets closer to Mid-America—is forcing us to reinvent church and rethink theology. Unfortunately our seminaries are autobiographical, preparing persons to move into the narrow stream of whiteness and middle class. We must remember that 87% of the world's population is now non-white."[3]

Census takers also inform us that, based on current trends, it is expected that sometime between 2040 and 2050 people of color will outnumber Caucasians in this country. I suspect this will be an "aha moment" for many. The oppressed in our society will be in the majority and white people in the minority. Things are certain to change then. So the church and society better get used to change and learn how to learn from each other. Churches used to appealing to white people must learn now how to work with diversity and with a variety of beliefs, rituals, and value systems.

Families Are Different

Fifty-four percent of Americans know a couple in which the woman is clearly the major wage earner and the man's career is secondary.[4] The number of racially or ethnically-mixed marriages has doubled since 1980. Our country has more than three million mixed marriages. William Frey points out that most of these involve young, well-educated members of higher income brackets.[5] Frey continues to explain the shift, when he writes, "Wealthy Hispanics are five times more likely to out marry than non-educated Hispanics."[6]

In a great work entitled *Becoming Family*, Robert Lauer cites statistics that indicate, "1 in 5 families with two parents in the home is a stepfamily."[7] "Between 7 and 8 million children under 18 are now living in stepfamilies."[8] Another study shows that 5.6 million grandparents live with their grandchildren, and 42 percent of them are responsible for their grandchildren. Thirty-six percent of grandparents have the children for at least five years.[9] And the number of unmarried adults living together out of wedlock increased 72 percent in the last decade.[10]

Divorcing before age thirty has become so common that it is creating a sociological phenomenon called starter marriages. Twenty-five percent of first marriages that end in divorce end in the first five years. And 20 percent of those divorces occur in the first two years.[11] America now has more single moms, more people living alone, and more people living together without blood or law connections than ever before.[12] In 1970 one million people were in "unmarried partner households," while by 2000 eleven million lived in such arrangements. Today's reality is that among Americans ages thirty-five to thirty-nine, many have lived in an "unmarried partner household."[13] About a third of children are born out of wedlock, and roughly the same percentage live with only one parent or neither parent.[14]

Single parent households have quadrupled since 1986. We now have in our nation nearly two million such families, making them the fastest-growing family type in the country.[15] Dr. James Dobson, in his book *Bringing Up Boys*, raises the following issues about the shifts in today's families: "Seventy percent of black babies and nineteen percent of white babies are born out of wedlock. Most will never know their fathers. Only thirty-four percent of children will live with both biological parents through 18 years of age. Sixty-two percent of mothers with children under three work outside the home."[16] He continues, "For the first time ever nuclear families dropped below twenty-five percent of all households, and households headed by unmarried parents increased by 72 per cent. Households headed by single mothers increased 25%, and those by single fathers grew by 62%."[17]

Marriage and family are now taking on another new twist. Since early 2004 the issue of gay marriage has been in the news across North America. Battles are raging in the political, educational, medical, and religious communities around this new reality in our culture. How will the outcome of this battle shift our culture?[18]

The church's beliefs about marriage and family may remain rooted in biblical teaching, but the families that present themselves to the church in its day-care programs, Bible study programs, and community outreach programs do not measure up to the church's cherished beliefs. How is the church to deal with this changed family situation? These issues will be addressed throughout the book.

Technology Is Different

Technology seems to be the driving force in much of the change in our culture The computer is making a greater impact on our culture than the printing press did in the days of Gutenberg. The advent of the computer brings the Internet, which, along with the proliferation of mobile phones, allows most of our culture to be accessible and connected to one another twenty-four/seven. Technology has fueled the rapid pace of change, communication, and advances in all areas of life and in all fields of public and private endeavor. Technology even fuels the economy, creating first the days of a bull market and then suddenly a bear market. We've enjoyed high tech's economic boom and now must endure its bust.

Medicine Is Different

Technological advances have also fueled advances in medicine. We are now living longer. The quality of life is greater for a longer period of time. This alone is creating challenges for social security, retirement, and job markets. It presents us the challenge of doing church with five to seven generations. Living longer has its challenges on many fronts, as well as its blessings.

Not only are these technological advances presenting longer life. They have also produced different possibilities of creating life. Cloning, designer babies, and genetic engineering are regular features in the news today. We're consumed by the possibilities of genetics and how they can alter life. This, of course, creates many ethical and religious challenges to the believer and thus to the church. This demands that the church have resources in its educational program to discuss intelligently the new technology and new genetic possibilities, along with their moral implications.

Generational Issues Are Different

With five to seven generations of persons living at one time, we find that each one has different learning styles and personal preferences (see appendix 1). Such generational issues present more challenges to the church and generate more intense dialogue than most any other cultural shift. How can the church minister effectively to all generations without alienating or ignoring one or more? What needs to happen in the church to attract, assimilate, disciple, and deploy each generation? Such critical issues face today's and tomorrow's religious leaders.

Education Is Different

The influx of technology, of various cultures, and of people groups have joined with the challenges of science, evolution, new lifestyles, and confused gender roles to produce radical shifts in the education system. Technology's sound bytes have created a generation with new learning styles. Home schooling is practiced in most communities on an increasing basis. School systems are faced with dual-language families and with learning to respect, preserve, and incorporate multicultural issues into curricula. Technology brings new types of classrooms and even new locations for classrooms. Traditional classrooms are now shifting to online learning opportunities for persons of all ages. People go to school and do their library research right from their personal home computer. This forces new economic issues and demands on already-overloaded school systems. All the while the challenges of the teaching profession increase as many families and communities look to the school to "raise their children" because they are in dual-career marriages or in a single-parent home. The church is also an educational institution and must face many of these same differences and challenges in our technological age.

Belief Systems Are Different

Wade Clark Roof suggests that "unlike old established religious denominations, popular religious culture is more diffused, less contained by formal religious structures." At the level of popular belief, Roof concludes, "we observe an eclectic mix of religious and spiritual ideas, beliefs, and practices. The success of this 'eclectic mix' of ideas is not due to its being 'institutionalized.' Rather these once-exotic but now commonplace notions have pursued a different route into public consciousness."[19] Of the world's two billion Christians, 560 million of them reside in Europe (though in dwindling churches). By 2025, Europe's Christian population is expected to remain unchanged, while the number of believers is expected to grow to 633 million in Africa, 640 million in South America, and 460 million in Asia.[20]

The World Is Different

President Bush has declared since the events of September 11, 2001, that the world is living in a "new normal." Threats of terrorism and implications of the tensions of diversity are generating challenges our world has not known before. Lessons to be learned, and challenges to be embraced and worked through seem to be the priority of our day. A sense of urgency, yet a sense of fear and anxiety, accompanies these challenges. This sense calls for skilled and courageous leaders who have a strong gift of discernment, a deep faith in God, and a focused ability in decision making. Our world's increasing diversity creates great challenge and opportunity. How will the church respond to the "new normal" of our world? Will we be a bridge builder or a barrier builder?

Church—Is It for Us or Them?

With all this diversity and the growing reality that most in our country are considered unchurched, what's the church to do? How can we effectively manage the present *and* effectively birth the future? We can't ignore the biblical mandate for the people of God found in our Great Commission (Mt. 28:18–20). We are "to go into all the world" and as we go "teach, preach and baptize." But we go and teach in a world radically different from that most current church leaders have ever known–for most of our current church leaders were born prior to 1955. Persons from this generation basically grew up in a church culture in which church was basically done for those inside the church family and inside the church walls. We paid our money for others to do the mission work. *Now* the world has come to our communities with all its diversity, and we are no longer in a church culture. The church must go and teach in a postmodern or secular culture. Many are asking, "Is the church for 'us' (those of us inside the church family) or is the church for 'them' (those not in the church walls or family)?" It seems to me this is one of the pivotal questions that spiritual leaders must confront in a secular age if the church is to survive and thrive in the next generation.

The Church Needs Leadership

With the challenges facing the church, its future depends on the courageous leadership of church leaders. Andy Stanley suggests two best-kept secrets about leadership:

1. The less you do, the more you accomplish.
2. The less you do, the more you enable others to accomplish.

Stanley reminds us that in Acts 6:1–7 the job eventually outgrew those closest to Jesus. Administrative activities consumed more and more of their time even when they were not necessarily good at it. Their administrative style divided the church. The new culture group joining the church accused the apostles of being too partial to Hebraic Jews. At some point the apostles realized things had to change. The mission of the church was at risk. The main thing was no longer their main thing. So they called a meeting.

Pay close attention to their opening statement, "It would not be right for us to neglect the ministry of the word of God in order to wait on tables" (v. 2, NIV).In other words, "We would be doing the wrong thing to continue caring for the widows ourselves." This awareness let them to appoint seven men who were equipped to handle this task. The apostles did not shirk their responsibility by doing this. On the contrary, they ensured that the job would be done better than before. New leaders surfaced, and more effective ministry was enjoyed. The apostles tried to do less and accomplish more by enabling others to accomplish more.[21] Stanley raises another issue of importance for the next generation of leaders when he declares, "the most productive people I know seem to have more, not less, discretionary time than the average person. They control their schedules rather than allowing their schedules to control them."[22]

These principles, along with others we'll explore, provide a foundation for courageous leadership that will move the church forward in the rapidly changing world of the twenty-first century.

Coaching questions are designed to help you focus and spread your leadership base to ensure more effective ministry.

Coaching Questions

After reviewing this brief summary of cultural shifts, consider the following:

1. On a scale of one to five (one being the least impact to five being the most impact) assess how each reviewed shift is already impacting your church and leadership?

2. Which one shift do your key leaders most often highlight?
3. What is preventing you from working with this new reality?
4. What will it take to begin to work with this issue more effectively?
5. When will you begin, and who can help you in this forward movement?

If you cannot answer one or more of these questions, keep reading. In the following chapters, we will help you find how and where to find answers.

2

Facing Reality
Looking into the Mirror

Leadership Challenges

"What causes our church to lose membership while our community is growing rapidly?"

"How can we help our church leaders and membership learn to embrace people who are not like us?"

"What are the dimensions of our church ministry that builds barriers to the unchurched and the postmodern world?"

"What can we do to move the church toward greater effectiveness of ministry in a postmodern and secular world?"

Learning to be a spiritual leader in a secular age is filled with challenges. Let me clarify again what I mean when I use the words *secular* and *postmodern* in this text. I'm using them to distinguish between the church culture and the secular or postmodern culture. That is, those who were born prior to the late 1950s basically grew up when most around them had some working knowledge and appreciation of (if not participation in) some church—thus a church culture. That is no longer the case. Today, most know little about traditional church, but many are on a spiritual journey—which most often does not connect with institutional church—and are thus part of a secular culture. Some would call these persons "postmoderns." Others are saying the world is moving beyond the postmodern age. However, the church hasn't even embraced the postmodern world. Many of our churches continue to be satisfied with living in the agricultural world and modern mindset—thus alienating many of them from the emerging world.

Cultural shifts only represent part of this challenge. Often a more stressful challenge is to look at actual current realities rather than perceived realities. For the first time in history many churches have the potential of reaching five generations. Churches and communities are learning to deal with generational distinctives and with the shifts these generations create in organizations, marketing, economics, businesses, academia, and church life. Sometimes it's really difficult for churches or leaders of one culture to see any value in the world that is different from that with which they are most familiar and comfortable. This is similar to my being out of place and somewhat stressed by being transplanted to a new home in the mountains and having to learn a different culture associated with living in the mountains. The landscape has not only shifted for me but for many in our world. Such change has created layers of challenge for Christians and for the institutional church. While some churches are struggling today with these shifts, other churches seem to have figured this new world out, and their churches are flourishing. Many of these are newly planted congregations. They are more open to change and challenge. They are reaching and discipling people effectively. On the other hand, many traditional congregations are have plateaued or are dying because they are not flexible and open to change or to much challenge. Some of these established churches are turnaround churches, and have moved from an ingrown church to an outgrown church. We'll deal with these churches in the next chapter. But for now, how do leaders and churches become more self-aware and more effective in their ministry as they face the new realities of a new world? What are some tools and strategies that have been used effectively to move churches and leaders forward? The first step and the most difficult step is looking into the mirror. Most leaders and churches avoid facing reality because the reality is most likely something they themselves have created.

Looking into the Mirror

An Initial Assessment—A Personal and Professional Shift

I continue to experience challenges as I learn to be an effective minister and consultant in this changing world. While I value my seminary training, I confess I continually have to unlearn things that had worked in a church culture so that I can learn strategies that are more effective in a secular culture. The unlearning is often the greatest challenge for me and opens up new learning curves and growth areas in my faith and my function as a consultant and coach. Only after I embraced these challenges to unlearn and learn anew did God restore unto me the joy and excitement of ministry in this secular culture.

Several years ago God started opening the doors for me to publish books–something I had never aspired to or even considered. Yet persons I was teaching in seminars wanted my materials. Publishing in print and on the Web seemed to be logical, but I did not have a clue about either. My first book, *Making the Church Work: Converting the Church for the 21st Century*, came out of my journaling as I learned to help leaders change values (that worked in one culture) so they could change structures (into ones that would work in a new culture). The book went into its second printing! Wow. Then I faced the Web with fear and trembling, but recognized it as a way of continuing to resource and network leaders and churches facing transition issues and challenges. One year after my first book was released, I ventured to put up my personal Web site–www.transformingsolutions.org – and to distribute two online newsletters. One is for deacons, and another is for other church leaders who are seeking coaching help to move them forward to a more effective ministry in this changing culture. God has used these newsletters far beyond my dreams.

During this time I was reframing my work as a consultant with the Baptist State Convention of North Carolina. Much of my work shifted from teaching the masses in seminar settings that were, for the most part, a "ya'll come" event. (I'm from the South, so I'll translate for others.) A "ya'll come" event is when a seminar is publicized as being open to whoever wants to come. While there's value in this, the seminars didn't seem to bear much lasting fruit for transitioning churches. So I did a few such events for the purpose of discovering the remnant–those persons or churches that gave evidence they were looking for and ready to take next steps in the journey of transitioning. I would then invite these leaders to a learning community. This community was invited and selected because of common affinity issues, and was nongeographical for the most part.

I simply invited the leaders to come together into a peer learning community to share their journeys in transitioning churches. This was a great experience! The learning was multidimensional, and God-blessed. I started with one learning community. As others heard about this community, we created others. I taught some members of our staff to create learning communities in their arenas of ministry. This represented a major shift in the way I did my work, but its value became clear as the fruit began to emerge. Now another shift is occurring as I begin to offer training without travel requirements, through teleclasses and online forums for leaders. Such new challenges have stretched me, but I quickly discovered that transformed leaders can and will transform churches and organizations.

Part of my personal transformation was a commitment I made to learn how to communicate the Good News to postmodern unchurched persons. I realized I had been writing and speaking about the unchurched, but I really did not know any. This commitment has evolved over thirteen years to be a part of my life where I see and experience God doing the neatest things, and in which God restores my hope for the church and for the world as I see postmodern persons finding and experiencing God in their secular world. My third book, *Reframing Spiritual Formation: Discipleship in an Unchurched Culture,* outlines the principles learned and the shifts I've been called upon to make as a Christian educator in a secular world.

These same principles provide the framework for this chapter as I share resources these groups have found most helpful in their journey. Many of those in the learning communities have discovered that they, too, needed to unlearn some things learned in a previous culture and reinvent themselves, their staff, their practices, sermons, and organizational structures to be more effective in reaching a new generation. We also discovered much about the need to manage the present while birthing the future. Sound interesting and challenging? You bet it is! Want to join our learning community? Okay, then. Let's move to the next step to provide you some tools for your journey.

Possible Tools for Your Journey

Cyberspace and the Internet form a major piece of our new reality. Many assessment tools and resources are available online. Leaders and congregations can utilize these to help them do some self-assessment. Certain generations and types of leaders might be more comfortable exploring and assessing themselves and their congregations via the Internet. Some of the most helpful sites for me are:

- www.easumbandy.com provides a framework for evaluating churches, leaders, and culture through three distinct types or groupings : Track 1–Church Renewal; Track 2–Growing Faith Community; Track 3–Mission Movement.
- www.ssjtutorial.org provides excellent assessment tools for redevelopment of congregations. This "spiritual strategic journey" was designed by Dr. George Bullard, executive coach for Lake Hickory Learning Communities, and was incorporated into the Alban Institute Web site www.alban.org
- www.pursuingvitalministry.org reviews the coach approach process of leadership development and congregational redevelopment. This approach is primarily designed to move churches forward from a plateaued position.
- www.gallup.com reviews the research of the George Gallup organization.

These are only representative. Check out my personal Web site, www.transformingsolutions.org, for an updated list of resources designed to help churches and leaders in transition and for many more options and tools.

Other leaders and churches are not Internet-friendly and desire printed resources. Personal assessment inventories provide a framework for dialogue among themselves as leaders, and with the congregations they serve. The resources, whether Web-based or in print, generate fruit-bearing dialogue as your leadership group becomes a learning community in which you help each other in the transformation and reinventing process. Support for the journey and tools to help lift the fog and clear the mirror of reality are essential. Too often leaders want to protect what we have helped birth and are thus not able to see clearly. These tools and the learning community help us to see clearly and not avoid things we might like to ignore or avoid.

Taking the first step of redeveloping a leader or congregation is often difficult, so it's best to do some preliminary assessment just to find some categories you might want to work with in further dialogues and explorations. This tool comes from the spiritual strategic journey Web site.[1]

Finding and Taking First Steps

You can begin to wade into the waters of reality and self-discovery by working through some preliminary questions before you engage in a renewal or reformation process as you transition from where you are to where God will be leading. God is always about creating something new, and it's good to remember that, as shown by the example of the beginning of creation, God often creates best out of chaos. So when things get messy, just know the new is being birthed. Complete the following initial assessment, and read the coaching notes related to the initial assessment.

The spiritual strategic journey is an intentional approach to reviewing the past, present, and future of a congregation through the lens of a group's spiritual journey of discerning and following the will of God for a given time in history. This approach isn't for every leader or church. For those seeking to begin by revisiting some spiritual foundations and thinking strategically as they learn about living into their future story, this is the appropriate plan. Others will not be so interested in such a systemic approach. They may be looking at things from a generational perspective as they desire to understand what's working and what's not working in their church.

It is not uncommon for me to have a conversation with a pastor or key leader who is seeking help to stop the bleeding in a congregation. I hear questions and comments such as the following:

- "How can I stop the bleeding on my membership rolls? I'm burying more of our faithful members each month than we are able to replace by reaching newcomers to bring into our community."
- "Our financial base is dwindling because of the decline of our membership and the deaths of our faithful tithers, while the maintenance demands of our facilities are growing with the age of our buildings. How can I stop the bleeding?"
- "We just don't have enough leaders to do what we need to do. Our leaders are aging out, and the younger people we do have aren't interested in or committed enough to carry on with the program and leadership demands. How can I deal with this reality?"

Questions like these are prevalent among many churches. The solution to every problem is found in acknowledging the reality of the situation. Solutions are found by naming the realities, not by playing a guessing game or following one's emotions. The truth here is that you cannot change what you do not acknowledge. Subjective approaches usually only fuel denial and avoidance. Often when you only guess or follow emotions, the situation continues to spiral downward.

The following inventories and strategies have worked to help many congregations find answers for the issues mentioned earlier. Review the tools. Discuss which tool might be best for your leadership core and congregation. Then dig in! This text will help coach you through the self-assessment and designing strategies that will strengthen your ministry in a secular age.

Congregational Initial Assessment

(Please rate your congregation on a scale of 1 to 5 on each of the following statements. An answer as low as 1 would mean that your congregation is not reflective of the statement. An answer as high as 5 would mean that your congregation is highly reflective of the statement. Answers in between these two extremes would suggest the relative agreement or disagreement you have with each statement when you think about your congregation.)

1. _____ Our congregation has a strong, clear, and passionate sense of our identity (who we are), our core values (what we believe or highly value), our vision (where we are headed), and our spiritual strategic journey as a congregation (how we are getting there).

2. _____ Our congregation is doing well at helping people connected with our congregation to be on an intentional and maturing faith journey. Among the results of the faith journey of people in our congregation is a deepening spirituality, the development of numerous new leaders, and a willingness by many people to get actively involved in congregational leadership positions and in places of ministry service through the congregation and beyond the congregation.

3. _____ Our congregation has some outstanding programs, ministries, and activities for which we are well known throughout our community. Our programs, ministries, and activities seem to be growing in numbers and quality. Our programs are meeting real, identified spiritual needs of people.

4. _____ Our congregation has excellent, flexible management systems (teams, committees, councils, boards) that empower the future direction of our congregation rather than seek to control the future direction. Decision-making is open and responsive to congregational input. Finances are healthy and increasing each year. The management systems are supportive of the visionary leadership efforts by the pastor, staff, and congregational leadership.

5. _____ Our congregation is demographically similar to its geographic community or the target groups that it has served

over the years. Little or no gap is developing between the persons attending our congregation and the geographic community or the target groups we have sought to serve over the past ten years. We are demographically reflective of the people we seek to serve in gender, age, race/ethnicity, socioeconomics, and lifestyle.

6._____ I can name at least seven people or 7 percent—whichever is higher—of the average number of active, attending adults in our congregation, present on a typical weekend for worship, who have a passionate sense of urgency for change and transition that may lead to transformation and the achievement of the full potential of our congregation.

7._____ Our congregation has grown in membership and weekly worship attendance over the past five to ten years by at minimum of 10 to 15 percent over that span of time.

8._____ Our pastor has a genuine commitment to change and transition for our congregation, which may lead to transformation and the achievement of the full potential of our congregation. In addition, our pastor is well respected by our congregation, and the congregation will proactively support our pastor's leadership in a congregational redevelopment effort.

9._____ Our key lay leaders have a genuine commitment to change and transition for our congregation that may lead to transformation and the achievement of the full potential of our congregation. In addition, our congregation respects them greatly, and the congregation will proactively support their leadership in a congregational redevelopment effort.

10._____ Our congregation has clear, open, healthy communication channels that allow the congregation to identify any issues that might disrupt the sense of fellowship and community. Our congregation works hard on healthy relationships. We know how to disagree without being disagreeable.

_____ TOTAL NUMBER OF POINTS

How did you do with the initial inventory? What new discoveries did you make about yourself? your congregation? Completion of this assessment is likely to provide excellent points for dialogue with other leaders in your congregation, and eventually with congregational members. What are the places on which most agreed? What are the places of greatest disagreements? How would you explain these discrepancies? What is needed to help each group understand the other's position or value system about how they perceive and experience church?

Coaching Notes on Congregational Initial Assessment

A score of 80 or higher probably indicates that your congregation does not need to engage in a congregational redevelopment process. It may already be on a significant spiritual, strategic journey that does not call for the amount of change and transition that would be part of a redevelopment effort.

A score of 40 to 79 probably indicates that your congregation is ready for a congregational redevelopment process. It may have a healthy level of openness to change and transition that could lead to transformation. It has a mindset that is open to a redevelopment effort.

A score of 39 or lower probably means that your congregation needs to engage in some readiness activities before attempting a congregational redevelopment process. This does not diminish its need or the urgency for redevelopment. It only indicates that some additional spiritual, strategic, and leadership readiness must be achieved before a redevelopment effort would be successful.

Go to www.ssjtutorial.org for further guidance following this strategic approach, regardless of where your church falls in the assessment scale.

Now we can move to the next step of congregational awareness. The next tool will help you select the most effective tool for moving your congregation forward. This is based on their preferred learning style. Finding the right process and design for growing the leaders and organization forward is critical. The following assessment can give you a clearer picture of how to proceed as you evaluate the effectiveness of your church's ministry in a secular culture.

Redevelopment Initial Assessment

(Please rank the statements below according to which statement best reflects the approach your pastor and congregational leadership would take to a congregational redevelopment effort. Rank your first choice as 1, your second as 2, your third as 3, and your fourth as 4.)

1. _____ Our congregation would prefer an approach that looks first at short-term, specific goals and actions we can begin taking.

Once we begin to see how these will work, we would then explore longer-term efforts at a more complete redevelopment process. This would be similar to a tactical planning approach. (Suggest that for your church an *incremental model* might be best to move you toward greater efficiency.)

2. _____ Our congregation desires to engage in a wholistic approach to redevelopment that takes a systemic look at our congregation and its context and builds on a traditional strategic planning model. (Suggest that for your church a *systemic model* might be best as you explore *big, holy, almighty* goals together.)

3. _____ Our congregation is very concerned about meaning, vision, and values. We have dreams concerning the future that we want to explore by engaging our congregation in telling the story of the future of our congregation that is emerging under God's leadership. (Suggest that for your church a *vision/values model* might be best as you craft together the future story of the congregation.)

4. _____ Our congregation likes to take action that is exciting and empowering and then reflect on the meaning of this action for our congregation. We are spontaneous. We are not bound by our heritage and traditions. Formal planning processes seem boring. (Suggest that for your church a *greatest experiences model* might be best as you recapture and celebrate the greatest experiences of the congregation.)

Learning the way the congregation learns and processes information best is very helpful as you move forward in planning and dealing with change. For additional information on each approach and model, go to www.ssjtutorial.com. This online approach may not be best for you as a leader or congregation. For instance, I had a pastor call who wanted to try to stop the bleeding in his congregation. He was very clear that much of what they needed to deal with as a congregation was the disconnect between who was inside the church walls and who was moving into the community. The members inside were over sixty; the people moving into new starter homes in the community were under forty. Generational issues seemed to be a very appropriate way to help this congregation. The trouble spots were not around vision, for they could see the future. Though some wanted to recapture the "good old days," many just wanted to reach the younger generation. Unfortunately, what they were trying had not worked. The community newcomers visited one time and then never returned. They were a very friendly church and just didn't understand why the younger generation did not want to join their fellowship. The following approach helped this congregation discover some new realties and build structures and values that not only attracted a new generation, but discipled and assimilated them into leadership very effectively.

Generational Approach to Moving Your Church Forward

While medicine and better health practices are keeping us alive longer and the growing diversity of people groups and cultures are multiplying, the church faces challenges we've never known. How do you minister effectively amidst such diversity? How can we get at this awesome challenge in a simple way? I recently had several exciting experiences while working with churches around the topic, "Keeping People Over 60 While Reaching People Under 40."[2] As part of this seminar, I shared something of the challenges the church is facing and then interviewed an unchurched friend from the postmodern world. I also created a safe place for church leaders and the postmodern unchurched person to dialogue in a question and answer session. In every situation following the dialogue, grandmothers and grandfathers, or parents of teenage and young adult children, would come up and thank us for the dialogue. They would declare, usually with tears in their eyes, that for the first time they were beginning to understand their children or grandchildren. Coming to understand various traits and values of each generation tends to open persons up to new understandings and experiences of the heart rather than fighting to make everybody in the world "like us."

The charts on pages 24–25 help provide succinct information about generational influences and distinctives. Once again I will provide some coaching questions designed to help leaders begin to process the information in light of your realities, not just your emotions. Working with these coaching questions can help with dogmatic opinions, distorted perceptions, confused value systems, and with an examination of personal preferences. Such information provides a backdrop for dialogue around the coaching questions provided here.

Coaching Questions about What You See in the Mirror

To this point we have introduced leaders and congregations to some tools to help assess reality. The challenge of a spiritual leader in a secular age is to deal with reality not just perception of reality. So

Contrasting the Generations—Three Generations in U.S. Society Today

	TRADITIONALISTS "The Silent Generation"	BOOMERS "Yippies"	X'ERS "Yiffies"
Birth Years	1925–1945	1946–1964	1965–1980
Conditioning Years	1930s–'40s	1950s–'60s	1970s–'80s
World Frame	Depression; WWII struggle and sacrifice; Delayed gratification	Sexual revolution; Economic expansion; Abundance; Spending	MTV; AIDS epidemic; Cynical; Grim economic reality
Family Structure	Nuclear	Divorced	Latchkey kids
Who, What Is Trusted	Doctors	Feelings	Technology
Music Favored	Swing; Old standards; "Elevator music" Rock and Roll;	Rock and Roll; Jazz; New Age	Rap; Punk; Heavy Metal; Alternative
Work Ethic	Work hard; Pay dues; Keep head down; "I am my job"	Climb the ladder; Build career; Workaholics; "Work is my life"	Distrust big business; Nine to five; Independence; "Work gives me life"
Attitude toward Authority	Respect it	Question it	Challenge it
Management Style Favored	Command and control	Collaborative	Entrepreneurial
Loyalty to	My company	My profession	My family
Organizational Structure Favored	Formal; Hierarchical	Informal; Accessible	Unconventional; Connected network

	TRADITIONALISTS "The Silent Generation"	BOOMERS "Yippies"	X'ERS "Yiffies"
How Job Is Valued	Stability; Security	Career growth	Stepping stone
How Communication Is Perceived	No news is good news	Any news is good news	Need news, straight talk, and feedback
How Organizational Life Is Dealt With	Dedicated; Committed; Social contract	Disillusioned; Downsized; Broken agreement	Realistic; Risk takers; No agreement
What Is Resented	Change; Lack of respect	Control; Slackers	Corporate politics; Boomers clogging the system
What Is Valued	Stability; Respect; Trust; Hard work; Loyalty	Variety; Achievement; Actualization; Career; Flexibility	Learning; Quality of life; Involvement; Stimulation; Fun

Sources: "Why Busters Hate Boomers," *Fortune* (October 4, 1993); Jane Bryant Quinn, "The Luck of the X'ers," *Newsweek* (June 6, 1994); "More Light on Generation X–The Psychological Contract," *Training* (May 1994); Bob Filipczak, "It's Just a Job," *Training* (April 1994); Kim McAlister, "The X Generation," *HR Magazine* (May 1994). From *The Heart of Coaching* by Thomas Crane (San Francisco: FTA Press, 2002), 155.

often leaders and congregations make decisions based on feelings–fears, comfort zones, likes, dislikes–more than the realities of a situation. For instance, many churches select music and design worship services around their likes, dislikes, and comfort zones, while at the same time saying they want to reach others (who more often than not do not share the same preferences). Such a disconnect creates many barriers instead of bridges and very often creates tensions for all concerned.

What disconnects and discoveries have you uncovered as you looked into the mirror through the previous tools and inventories?

Take another step in self-discovery after a careful review and discussion of the generational issues reflected in these charts:

1. What are the disconnects between the way you and your church are currently functioning in practice and belief and what the chart suggests?

   ILLUSTRATION: In one of my recent consultations this chart and coaching question helped a church discover and acknowledge that they said they wanted to reach younger persons but that they didn't create any short-term, hands-on opportunities for these newcomers to engage in leadership and mission involvement. The existing generation of leaders, from the silent generation, were trying to be loyal to their historical program and committee traditions, and the younger generation couldn't get into leadership or missions because of the discrepancies of values and lack of structures that were entry points for a new generation.

2. What generational groups comprise your current leadership and tithing base? What did you learn from your review of the chart in light of these realties?

   ILLUSTRATION: One group discovered that more than 70 percent of their current church leaders were older than sixty. This same church discovered that 80 percent of their current tithers were older than sixty. They could not find much evidence of the younger generation moving into either group. What an "aha" for this church. This insight alone motivated them to think more strategically of how to build mentoring relationships between the old and the young and how to incorporate leadership training and gift discovery into their outreach and assimilation efforts with the younger generation.

Reflection Time: Gaining Perspective on the Journey

Coaching questions are about helping people make informed decisions and build ownership of those decisions so decisions are not imposed by outsiders, but rather discovered by those involved in the situation. Coaching is also all about moving a person or organization into the future as a stronger, more confident and effective leader and church. What have you discovered thus far as you discover new realities, look carefully into the mirror, and experience the lifting of the fog that has been covering the beauty of God's creation?

Since coaching is about moving people forward in faith and function, adjustments and decisions are called for but not imposed. God calls the church to make adjustments to line up with God and to move away from those things that weigh us down. I am simply trying to assist you to determine what's preventing you as a leader or organization from being as effective as God desires in a world that is rapidly changing. I am not suggesting that you compromise your biblical values. I do hope you may be encouraged to examine your personal preferences or generational differences that might be barriers to effectiveness. Are you ready to press on?

1. What are some adjustments in belief or practice that seem to be suggested? What are the steps of making these adjustments?
2. What are you willing to do and by when?

Embracing the New—Hope for a New Generation

I am more convinced than ever that God is going to use the church to accomplish the divine purpose in the world—even this crazy and changing world. I am equally convinced that not every building with a steeple is God's church, concerned about God's mission. Many of our churches are much more concerned about *their* agendas than they are about God's agenda. Many of our leaders are more concerned about their comfort than they are about becoming a people on mission with God in the world. The churches that God seems to be blessing and using most effectively in this culture are those places that are willing to grow, be flexible, and be open to change. These churches are learning to embrace the new rather than cling to the past. I'll discuss this further in chapter 9.

What will it take to embrace the new so we might be more effective in sharing the good news with another generation? What will it take to become more open to change and mission and God's agenda? Abraham and Sarah were very open to God's agenda even into their eighties. When God told them to move to "a land that I will shew thee," (Gen. 12:1, KJV) a land unfamiliar to them, they moved! We can do no less as we try to be found faithful people of God reaching a new generation.

Leaders and congregations who feel stuck and unable to reach a new generation and who really want to continue to be faithful to the Great Commandment and the Great Commission usually feel such a pinch that they are ready to consider other options. Leaders and congregations who choose to live in comfort or denial about their reality will likely die after the current generation ages out. Those who choose to walk into their fears and strengthen their faith can help pioneer doing church among the new generation. Becoming aware of generational distinctives is certainly a significant issue of becoming more self-aware and seeing reality more clearly. Another piece of reality also needs some reflection. This moves around the issue of how generations see and respond to leadership. Use the summary chart "Leadership and Five Generations" found in appendix 1 as another opportunity for assessing reality and planning next steps.

Coaching Questions about Your Reflections

Based on your reflection on appendix 1 and previous material, talk with your peers about the following:

1. What are the issues that create an "aha" experience (an insight where new reality is discovered and embraced as the fog lifts and new realities emerge) for you as you review generational distinctives and how they might be reflected in your church leadership, programming, or values (values relate to one's personal preferences and comfort zones)?

   ILLUSTRATION: A church trying to reach younger persons when the primary decision makers in the church are all of the builder generation is likely to have issues unless thedifferent age groups understand each other clearly. The chart suggests that the builder generation endures when it comes to authority. They are likely to believe and act as though this younger generation should just "do what we say." Again, the chart is clear that the "nexter" generation *chooses* whom they will follow. They choose based on relationships and respect of purpose, not because they are told to respect or follow.

2. How would you communicate the discrepancies you are seeing or experiencing to others in your leadership group?

   ILLUSTRATION: The value of exploring the charts about generations and looking for discrepancies in the way your organization supports or challenges each generational distinctive can allow you to find some of those issues that might be preventing a congregation from effectively reaching a new generation and provide some guidance about how adjustments might be made in mindsets or structures to more effectively relate to other groups.

3. After examining carefully the generational charts and issues in your congregation, what truths become clear for you about where you *are* and where you *want to be* as a leader or congregation?

4. How can you move from where you are to where you want to be? Consider shifts that might be indicated by another review of the charts.

Such a glance into the mirror of reality is certain to create some tension for individuals, and often the congregation, as discrepancies between word and deed begin to appear. Helping persons verbalize these disconnects and how they feel about them and why they feel the way they do is a valuable exercise that frequently creates understanding, builds ownership of the new vision, and helps all concerned find and take next steps. So keep talking through the discoveries and the disconnects. Then begin to pray together about them. Not everyone will agree on all discoveries or disconnects. That is okay. What we know is that you can change the culture of a church if you can get 20 to 25 percent of the active adults to embrace a new idea. What you are working to discover is God's leadership for your congregation. Often this emerges out of such a reality check and honest dialogue and prayer. Also, some generational distinctives might emerge that the church can continue to explore together.

Just as each generation and culture possesses some unique characteristics, so also certain leadership styles bear more fruit in certain groupings than other groupings of persons. Let's review briefly leadership style distinctives as a way of looking into your mirror. What leadership styles are most prevalent in your situation? What style are you most comfortable/uncomfortable with? What shifts might be called for, and what are you willing to do about these discovered realities?

Shifts in Reality Begin with Leadership Style

New generations and new cultures call for new leadership styles among leaders and organizations. Reality shows have become popular in the last few years. They depict real people in real time engaged in real life situations in public ways. Such a trend represents a significant shift from the shows I grew up with, such as *Leave It to Beaver* and *The Andy Griffith Show*. Then most leaders were elected or clearly recognized, and most episodes of the TV shows ended on a favorable note, at least suggesting that "they lived happily ever after." Reality today is just the opposite. Leaders are formal *and* informal leaders– visible and invisible. Most situations in real life are murky at best and more often than not do not end with all persons "living happily ever after." Recognizing such significant shifts, we must find ways to lead our people to cope and create a church family willing to incorporate such diversity of views and realities *if* we are to minister to "all the world." What are the lessons we might glean about leadership shifts that may be part of shifts we discover in our reality checks? How is leadership shifting in order to be more effective among our shifting culture and diversity of generations and people groups? How can the church embrace such shifts without compromising our biblical foundations? How can we retool to speak more effectively to multiple generations and challenges?

Ron Martoia has summarized these shifts and challenges succinctly. Martoia declares, "Leadership in this century is more about teams and communities than individuals." He also reminds us that, "None of us is as smart as all of us and control is out, connect and collaborate are in."[3] These phrases summarize significant shifts in leadership that are being called for in our new century, and capture the shifts we are facing and called upon to make.

Now think about your leadership style and church. Are you more into control or collaboration? (We'll deal more with this in chapters 10 and 11.) Are you more into individual leadership or team leadership models? While the shifts in leadership style are difficult, they seem more in keeping with biblical mandates for the community of faith. Such shifts again provide some insights about why some churches are effective and others are not as effective. Some generations respond to loyalty of institution for loyalty's sake. Other generations are not as loyal to institutions as they are to community and to a purpose they embrace and believe in, rather than purposes they are told to believe in or engage.

Martoia concludes that, "The fact is, times are changing and 'times' are the things that mold leaders."[4] This truth has profound implications for the church as we face the challenges of our secular age. What shifts can we embrace in leadership style and substance without compromising our biblical heritage? How can such shifts best be lived out?

Leadership for a New Generation

Leadership in a church culture has been based primarily on positions of elected or appointed leaders. Those in the culture followed or endured the leadership's direction. Now in a secular age, when religious leaders have been in the news almost daily because of moral failure of some kind, many of the secular generation are very cynical or skeptical of following any religious leader without questions being asked or leadership being earned. In the church culture leadership used to be more about such things as the following:

> ...finding the answers we needed. Now leadership *has become* more about finding and voicing the right questions in the right context at the right time.

> ...the skill set leaders possessed. Now leadership *has become* more about fully being, inhabiting my destiny, and having an inner morphic dynamic with God. Ron Martoia explains,

"Who I am creates a certain kind of feel and ethos in which people either thrive or attempt to survive. The ethos created is more important to transforming a life than learning a particular skill. Skill without ethos will lead to mechanical execution."[5]

...arriving at some out-there goal, taking a summit, or storming a hill. Now leadership *has become* more about crafting the present ethos, which is the organic soil of the emerging ministry tomorrow.

...serial sequencing. Now leadership *has become* about parallel simultaneity. Martoia reminds us, "The Jesus model of training was on the job."[6]

The point here is that leadership shifts are being called for due to generational, cultural, and societal norms, and due to new realities. The leadership model of Jesus had a real sense of fluidity and customization about it as he related at many different levels with a wide array of persons inside and outside the religious community. We are facing similar challenges to ensure our effectiveness in today's culture.

The remainder of this book will explore how these shifts are made and how they can best be manifest to reach a secular culture.

The Big Picture of New Realities

While this chapter is only a glimpse into the mirror of your organization and it's challenges, it's a good start. The big picture is a realistic assessment by key leaders of the primary focus, values, and function of your leaders and local congregation. Are you realistically structured, leading and programming for the groups you are desiring to reach? Or are there discrepancies that need to be addressed? If the church feels they are being faithful to biblical mandates for a New Testament church by what they are doing and how they are doing it, blessings on you. Press on. If you've been able to identify gaps between where you are and where you want to be, the journey of renewal and adjustment can continue. The remainder of this book will continue to provide stories of inspiration, guidance, and adjustments that many have made in order to be more effective in our current culture.

A final summary of all we've been unpacking is found in the chart "Are We a Mission or Maintenance Congregation?" on page 33. Explore each indicator of the value system of each of the respective churches. How do you see yourself? your congregation? The following chart is another great tool for helping you and your leaders take the data you've already discovered to the next and hopefully more practical and emotional level. Read carefully—maybe even pray through—the following chart created by Ronald Russell and found in the excellent book of his church's journey of redevelopment, *Can a Church Live Again?*[7]

Coaching Questions to Consider as You Work with the "Maintenance and Mission" Chart

1. How many issues in each column are true about you/your church?
2. What issues in each column are most frequently agreed upon and perceived by the most leaders in your congregation?
3. Who are the persons that might cluster around the issues of most concern?
4. What can these persons do with the issue they are most tuned into and passionate about that might help move the church forward toward a greater faithfulness and function in communicating the good news in an increasingly secular culture?

Looking beyond the Mirror

It's one thing for me to look into the mirror each morning. It's quite another thing to do something about what I see. If I didn't act on what I see, I would scare the world when I walked out of my house. Rather I must act and brush my teeth, shower, shave, comb my hair, and get ready for the world I will work in that particular day. Too often the church just looks into the mirror to see itself without asking about how to best prepare for the world in which it is planted. Now I want to nudge you to do a final piece of self-assessment and discovery about all that you have seen in the mirror. Look at your new information in light of what difference would all of this make in a primarily secular, pagan, postmodern world of people. Jesus left us to be in the world but not of the world. He left us to be salt, light, and leaven to impact the world. This part of the self-assessment is world-focused. How does what we've discovered and what shifts and callings we've decided to follow impact the gathered church and the scattered church that works and lives in the secular world during the week? The following chart again only summarizes and provides a guideline for dialogue about being spiritual leaders in a secular age. We'll continue to work on these concepts throughout the book.

Christian Leadership Impact on the Church and World

How do the characteristics of Christian leadership impact/influence the scattered and the gathered church?

Are We a Mission or Maintenance Congregation?

Maintenance Congregation	Mission Congregation
Worship style is the same as it was five years ago.	Worship styles change frequently to reflect new subcultures that the church is trying to reach.
Most adult Sunday school classes have not added anyone new in the last six months, and no new units have been added in the last year.	Adult Sunday school classes are more interested in telling the world about Jesus than they are in keeping things the way they are.
Bible study is geared toward information and scholarship.	Bible study is geared toward transformation and relationship.
Does its best not to offend any of the church members.	The mission is the thing. Willing to lose a few for the sake of winning larger numbers to Christ.
Keeps the same programs going year after year with little or no discussion about whether they are actually needed.	Is willing to scrap old programs and ways of doing things once they begin to lose their effectiveness.
Believes that new technology has no place in the church.	Sees technology as a tool to reach new generations for Christ. Is willing to add new technology.
Adopts a budget that is based on "what we did last year."	Adopts a budget based on what the congregation perceives God is up to now and next year.
Asks the question of new ideas, "How does this fit into our present programs?"	Asks the question of new ideas, "What is its disciple-making function?"
Evaluates how it is doing by comparing to other congregations.	Evaluates how it is doing by how many people are in ministry.
Bases success on how many people are coming to the church's events and programs.	Bases success on how many people are doing ministry outside the walls of the church.
Devotes a lot of energy and resources to keeping the church running smoothly.	Welcomes chaos and sees it as a sign that God is up to something.
Has a strong central governance with a recognizable chain of command.	Views everyone as involved in ministry. Ministry leaders exist to resource, support, and encourage those in ministry.
Looks very homogeneous on Sunday morning; i.e., everyone looks alike.	Is multicultural, multiracial, multiethnic, and accepting of everyone.
Membership is mostly made up of people from the same denominational background.	Has a diverse congregation made up of people from many denominations and religious backgrounds.
Focuses on requirements for church membership and making sure that everyone has the correct doctrine.	Focuses on making disciples who are moving toward becoming fully devoted followers of Jesus Christ.
Has very little sharing of hurts, habits, and hang-ups.	Welcomes the broken and offers a safe place for anyone who comes.

Christian Leadershp Impact on the Church and World

CHARACTERISTICS	CHURCH (Gathered Church)	WORLD (Scattered Church)
Visionary Skills (Prov. 29:18)	Guidance, focus, relevance, to ensure fulfillment of church's mission	Help ensure that redemptive purpose/ visions are part of business practices and decisions
Decision-Making Skills	Clear, focused decisions in meaning, making, and fulfilling church's mission	Integrates Christian privileges in business decisions and practices; Channel for witness
Relational Skills (Jn. 15)	Build community, servanthood, modeling, mentoring, incarnational ministries	Build community, servanthood, modeling, mentoring, incarnational ministries
Spiritual Gift/Discovery/ Use (Rom. 12:1, Eph. 4, 1 Cor. 12, 1 Pet. 2:9–10)	To facilitate fulfilling servanthood ministry within the life of the community of faith; To bring motivation and focus to mission and ministry	Ensures that work and faith have a place of integration; To enlighten others as to the work of Christ in and through one's daily life
Activation of the Fruit of the Spirit (Gal. 6) Love, Joy, Peace...	To represent Christ's presence in our midst; To activate growth areas in spiritual life formation	Provide opportunity to be church and be the presence of Christ in the world; Create opportunity for presence of Christ to be made known through who we are and in what we do

Coaching Questions after Reflecting on the Chart

1. How many of the insights/plans you've embraced during the work of this chapter have direct and powerful impact on the gathered church? on the scattered church?

2. What are the weak points of your decisions and commitments in light of learning to be and *do* church in a secular culture as the "scattered church"?
3. What might be done to strengthen your plans and commitments so that the good news might be communicated more effectively to all those who are on a spiritual journey but may not currently find their way into the gathered church community and programming?
4. What are you willing to do to make these adjustments?

This poem seems to be a fitting way to end this chapter. What is the Spirit saying to you after you've had a closer look into the mirror of your life, your community, and your congregation? What are the places and points where the Lord is disturbing you? What's your next step?

Disturb us, Lord, when
We are too well pleased with ourselves
When our dreams have come true
Because we dream too little,
When we arrive safely
Because we sailed too close to the shore.

Disturb us, Lord, when
With the abundance of things we possess
We have lost our thirst
For the waters of life;
Having fallen in love with life,
We have ceased to dream of eternity
And in our efforts to build a new earth,
We have allowed our vision
Of the new Heaven to dim.
Disturb us, Lord, to dare more boldly,
To venture on wider seas
Where storms will show your mastery;
Where losing sight of land,
We shall find the stars.
We ask You to push back
The horizons of our hopes;
And to push us in the future
In strength, courage, hope and love.
This we ask in the name of our Captain,
Who is Jesus Christ.[8]

3

When Maintenance Becomes the Mission

Leadership Challenges

"We have the friendliest church in town."

"We have the greatest pastor in town—he visits every member of the church on a regular basis, is available to us for emergencies, and visits faithfully when we have a death in the family or when someone's in the hospital."

"We have a great fellowship. We all know each other by names; we really don't need name tags, and we are always having fellowships that we all enjoy."

"We have a great building. It meets all our needs for worship, prayer, Bible study, recreation. We even have a church bus we use for fellowship trips."

Spiritual leaders *in* the church find the best and worst examples in many traditional churches. The values of the traditional church culture found focus and meaning in buildings, budgets, church growth, and church health. More often than not, these values and agendas became the mission for many local congregations. These churches quickly became ingrown rather than outgrown. We are now realizing that such a value system, though seemingly appropriate at the time of decision-making, moved many churches and church leaders into a maintenance mentality. The church became ingrown, more focused on preserving the institution, church value system, and preferences than moving ahead with God's mission in the world. It proved to be much safer, easier, and less messy to work within the church than in the world.

The consequence of this is fairly clear. In 2004 over 80 percent of most established churches have plateaued or are declining in participation and membership. It is estimated that about 65–70 percent of our population is now unchurched.[1] Our church culture membership is aging out, and most churches are not reaching persons under 40 years of age, primarily because their values and preferences are different from those of the traditional church. Postmoderns want to be on mission and are not interested in maintenance issues that they perceive to be the mission of most churches.

In a secular or postmodern culture many churches are being challenged to recapture the biblical mission instead of their ingrown mission of maintenance—the "business as usual" mentality. The postmodern world challenges churches to move from an inward focus (taking care of us) to an outward focus (reaching them). Often the challenge is to move from buildings, budgets, and church growth to decentralized communities of faith who give away resources rather than keeping them. The challenge may be on church effectiveness and efficiency rather than on church health or growth (not that they are exclusive of one another, but the focus is different). The postmodern culture wants to give their money to real people to meet real needs in real time. They want to go with their money rather than send it through institutions that many perceive as cold and self-serving.

The challenge becomes clear. Change is inevitable if a church expects to survive and be effective in a rapidly changing world. Ingrown churches not open to the "new thing God is doing" will gradually close their church doors.

Bethel Church was a wonderful fellowship of God-fearing people who had grown up together in the same community for decades. The church was the place of celebrations, fellowship, and care giving. Such a vision and function had been working just great for decades, but then the younger generation went away to college and never returned. The number of children quickly diminished in the little church. The number of younger couples became fewer and fewer, to the point that the church was no longer attracting the youth of the community. In fact, the community had no youth. The church had a good tithing base, so they were able to hire pastors to try to "save the church" from new cultural realities. The problem was that the demographics had shifted, but the current church leaders expected and even demanded that their pastors visit them regularly, take care of the sick, elderly, bereaved, and disgruntled in the church, *and* try to "save the church." Pastors came and went, for they burned out and decided they could not possibly fulfill all the leaders' expectations. The church was more concerned about maintenance issues than mission opportunities.

Calvary Church was just across the street and represented another denomination. They dealt with the same demographic realities, but their leaders decided that they wanted to be on mission and create a church for a new generation. They decided to address the needs of those not already in the church rather than just take care of the needs of those in current membership. Their pastors went about this mission, not just caring for those in the membership. This church flourished. Members were driving in from outside the little community, for the church was designed to reach them. The church started home cell groups in the communities outside their immediate community to make church more convenient for the newcomers.

The difference between the two churches is obvious. The difference lay in the focus of their mission and the priorities for their pastors, members, budgets, and programming.

When the mission becomes maintenance, what are the consequences? When spiritual leadership is manifested only *in* the church, the church frequently becomes inwardly focused and maintenance minded. It gradually begins to decline in number and effectiveness. What are the warning signs that such an inward focus is emerging? What are the basic steps of moving from maintenance to mission, from ingrown to outgrown? These questions give focus to the remainder of this chapter.

Warning Signs to Consider

My work with and in churches for over twenty years has produced a list of some of the warning signs that suggest a church's mission has become maintenance. Every church needs to check its values and its operation against this list.

A church's mission has become maintenance when

• the budget is more inward focused than outward focused

- church members' expectations about pastor and staff revolve more around care-giving for the members than around equipping the membership for mission and ministry
- church meeting agendas focus more on "our needs" than on "the needs of the unchurched or nonbelievers"
- most church groups, classes, and activities are "closed" to outsiders because they focus primarily on members and are not sensitive to needs of the nonmember
- the church creates few, if any, nonthreatening, comfortable entry points for the unchurched or nonbelievers
- multiple layers of management are implemented so as to monitor or control direction and focus of the church
- the church leadership's values can be summarized by "taking care of us" rather than "reaching them (the unchurched)"
- what we pray for and count are the persons in our membership rather than those we reach or touch from outside the fellowship
- we value preserving our church buildings and values more than penetrating the culture and community with the good news of Christ[2]

How many of these are "more true" than not about your congregation? If you have more than half of these as "more true" than not, you are moving in dangerous directions.

Consequences When Maintenance Becomes the Mission

When maintenance becomes the mission, the church reaps positive and negative consequences, depending on your perspective. Here are some positives from the perspective of many church members:

- Members' needs are a priority.
- Pastoral care is done primarily by pastor and paid staff.
- Budget goes to care for needs and desires of those who are members.
- Close "family ties" are nurtured and enjoyed.
- Language becomes familiar and clannish.
- Change is avoided.

But here are some negatives from the perspective of the unchurched community:

- The church ignores or minimizes our needs.
- The church ignores or minimizes our pastoral care needs.

- Financial resources do not appear available for our needs so we perceive the church as "those selfish church people who don't care about my needs."
- Closeness of church members becomes a barrier for the unchurched to become accepted or even "get into" the church family.
- Language often becomes a barrier instead of a bridge to finding and taking next steps in our spiritual journey.
- Barriers are perceived or created that perpetuate the "us and them" mentality and perspective.

Maintenance does not have to remain a church's mission. A church can recognize and acknowledge the problem. Until the problem is acknowledged, the problem cannot be resolved. Once the church faces reality, then the church is ready to change its mission.

Spiritual Leadership Shifts from *in* to *through* the Church

To move away from a mission of maintenance, spiritual leadership must shift from *in* the church to *through* the church. The first step is to find those in the congregation who are passionate about moving forward to be more faithful to the biblical mission and to move away from their personal agendas or preferences. Who are those persons? How might these persons begin to dialogue and pray together? (Be careful here! This group can easily become a "down on the church or staff group." It must instead remain a group encouraged by staff and church to focus and pray for forward movement in accomplishing the Great Commission.) Once this prayer and dialogue begins, other steps will likely emerge and call for action.

This group will not likely automatically know what to do. They will need coaching from the church leadership and staff.

The following coaching questions can help the group keep moving forward:

- What does God seem to be calling the church to become?
- What elements of church as we've known it seem to be out of line with God's biblical mandates?
- What can the group read and reflect on that might inform decision-making? (See suggested list at end of this chapter.)
- Who in the group shares common passions that need further exploration and study? (In other words, who are the persons in the church who seem to see the future and are willing to give energy to creating a future that is more effective than what they are experiencing in the present?)

- How can the group learn to build bridges rather than barriers between the churched and the unchurched?
- What are the gaps between what the church is now and what God is calling the church to become?
- How can this group help close or address some of these gaps?
- What other persons inside or outside the church might be able to help in closing or addressing these gaps?
- What is the group willing to do and by when?
- How will we know when we have achieved new focus and mission?

Achieving a new focus takes time and patience, but most of all it takes perseverance by a group who sees the vision and has the passion to make it happen. This group will need to share the vision with the entire congregation and invite them to amend, adjust, or adapt the vision as it continues to emerge.

Moving from maintenance to mission takes time, intentionality, dedication, and perseverance. It doesn't happen quickly, nor does it happen without discomfort, pain, struggle, and sometimes conflict. However, the journey is worth the effort if we really want to be a church that brings pleasure to our Heavenly Father and if we want to be faithful to the biblical mandates for the people of God. The journey is also filled with great excitement, joy, new life, and transformed lives as we align persons and congregations to the call of God upon our lives.

Lake Hickory Resources has a process in place to help in this effort of revitalizing your church. This process is about coaching the leaders and congregations through gaps and learning curves they identify for themselves as they begin to move from being spiritual leaders *in* the church to spiritual leaders *through* and *as* the church. Pursuing vital ministries is a coach approach to this shift in focus and organization. See www.pursuingvitalministries.org.

Outgrowing an Ingrown Church

A church with a maintenance mission is an ingrown church. This ingrown condition represents a serious church ailment that needs healing. Lyle Schaller, a nationally known church consultant, developed an assessment tool to help persons assess their congregation and their leaders. Take time to pray through and work through each question carefully in regards to your own congregation. Mark each statement that is applicable in your situation.

The following signals suggest that a numerically growing congregation is about to drift off onto a plateau in size or even to begin to experience a decline in numbers.

1. Taking better care of today's members moves ahead of evangelism and outreach to the unchurched on the local list of priorities.
2. The pastor spends more time thinking and talking about retirement a few years hence than being devoted to outreach and evangelism.
3. The number one issue on the current agenda is the resolution of conflict.
4. The average attendance at worship begins to drop when compared to the same months a year earlier.
5. The average attendance in Sunday school begins to decline.
6. The unhappy or involuntary termination of two consecutive pastors is followed by a plateau or decline in numbers.
7. The church experiences a succession of two-to-four-year pastorates.
8. The key signal often is a decrease in the number of households that underwrite most of the annual budget.
9. The number of new members received by letter or transfer or certificate from other churches declines.
10. The total compensation of the paid staff exceeds 50 percent of the total member contributions.
11. References to the past begin to overshadow plans, dreams, and hope for the future of this congregation.
12. A decrease occurs in the number of baptisms.
13. The new minister spends more time with individuals than with groups of people.
14. The net worth of all capital assets (land, building, cash reserves, investments) declines after full adjustments for inflation and depreciation.
15. At least one-half of today's members joined more than ten years ago.
16. Week after week, nearly everyone has disappeared within ten to twelve minutes after the benediction at the close of the last Sunday morning worship service.
17. The church cuts back on special worship services (Thanksgiving, Christmas Eve, Holy Week, special anniversaries, etc.).
18. The total dollars given for missions and benevolence drop.
19. The church is unable to design and implement a five-year plan for ministry, program, and outreach.

20. The proportion of teenagers from outside the membership who are regularly involved in youth ministries decreases.
21. Seniority, tenure, and kinship or friendship ties with members of the nominating committee often outweigh skill, wisdom, creativity, competence, experience in other congregations, or enthusiasm when the congregation is choosing policy makers for the coming year.
22. The ratio of worship attendance to membership drops year after year.
23. The response to an impending financial problem is to concentrate on reducing expenditures rather than on increasing dollar receipts.
24. The only significant increase in total receipts year after year is in rentals received for use of the real estate or in the size of the denominational subsidy or in income from the endowment fund.
25. The median age of the congregation rises steadily.
26. The church decides to cut back on program, the Sunday morning schedule, staff, finances, weekday programming, outreach, benevolence, or office hours.

Thriving churches today can become inward focused churches tomorrow without intentional spiritual leadership that seeks to move beyond an inward maintenance focus to mission. The traditional church's tendency to is to rest on a comfortable plateau in size and dream of something better for tomorrow. The best response to is to watch for these early warning signs and initiate preventive action.[3]

Coaching Questions for Leaders and Churches Who Discover They Are Ingrown or Have Plateaued

- What are the top three indicators of your ingrown nature as a church?
- Who inside or outside the church can help address these top three issues?
- Whom do you know who has influence on one or more of these factors/issues?
- How could you share your concern and observations with these persons?
- What can be done to help address the issues so you can move toward a more outward-focused culture?
- What are the possible barriers or obstacles you might encounter?
- How could you deal with those obstacles or barriers?
- What are you willing to do and by when?

• What initial results will indicate that you are making progress toward becoming a more outward-focused church?

Moving from maintenance to mission takes hard work. Such work requires retooled courageous leaders willing to face reality and press through personal and corporate comfort and discomfort. Spiritual leaders who primarily focus *in* the church limit themselves and the mission of the congregation. Spiritual leadership that emerges *through* the body of Christ energizes for mission. Spiritual leadership then begins to impact the culture *as* an agent of redemption and reconciliation. The next section deals with how spiritual leadership manifests itself *through* the body of Christ to rejuvenate leaders and organizations.

Suggested Resources for the Journey

Blackaby, Henry. *Spiritual Leadership.* Nashville: Lifeway, 2000.

Bullard, George, "Resource Guide for Spiritual Strategic Journey–Coach Approach to Congregational Development," available at www.congregationalresources.org/bullard.asp.

Carter, Bill. *Team Spirituality.* Nashville: Abingdon Press, 1997.

Coaching Congregations, available at www.coachingcongregations.com.

Easum, Bill. *Growing Spiritual Redwoods.* Nashville: Abingdon Press, 1997, available at www.easumbandy.com.

____. *UnFreezing Moves: Following Jesus into the Mission Field.* Nashville: Abingdon Press, 2001.

Hammett, Edward. *Making the Church Work: Converting the Church for the 21st Century.* Macon, Ga.: Smyth and Helwys, 1997, available at www.transformingsolutions.org.

Miller, C. John . *Outgrowing an Ingrown Church.* Nashville: Abingdon Press, 1986.

Net Results, available at www.netresults.org

Nixon, Paul. *Fling Open the Doors.* Nashville: Abingdon Press, 2002.

Ogden, Greg. *Transforming Discipleship.* Downer's Grove, Ill.: InterVarsity Press, 2003.

Russell, Ronald. *Can a Church Live Again?* Macon, Ga.: Smyth and Helwys, 2003, available at www.helwys.com.

Wilkes, C. Gene. *Jesus on Leadership.* Nashville: Lifeway Press, 2003.

____. *Paul on Leadership.* Nashville: Lifeway Press, 2004.

Wood, Gene. *Leading Turnaround Churches.* St. Charles, Ill.: ChurchSmart Resources, 2001.

WHERE WE WANT TO BE

Spiritual Leadership *through* the Church

4

The Mission
Finding Christ in Our Culture

Leadership Challenges

"The church has just lost its influence in our community. Instead of the church effecting the world, the world has influenced the church."

"With all these unmarried people shacking up and having babies out of wedlock, the church can't invite them to be part of our church."

"The decay of the traditional family is going to be the downfall of the church."

"The church can't possibly take care of all the poor and homeless; we have to take care of our own first. We don't have time or resources to help beyond our own membership."

Learning to mobilize the church in our culture is the challenge for most church leaders today. Some say our culture is plummeting to all-time lows, citing moral decay as a major barometer. Others suggest that instead of the church influencing the culture, the culture is impacting the church. Others say God can't be found in our pagan and increasingly secular culture. Others declare God is found in the midst of the culture; but the church has lost sight of God among the poor, the homeless, the broken places and broken people, and those places where injustice is found.

Richard Niebuhr addressed this issue in his classic book *Christ and Culture*.[1] One of the challenges the church of the twenty-first century has is to find Christ in our culture and learn to join Him and respond to Him and with Him there. The challenge of leadership and the church is clear–how do we move from being apart from the culture to finding God amidst the culture? If we are trying to move from where we are to where we want to be, we as leaders face the challenge of addressing this question first within ourselves. Then we must model a solution through the lives we live out before the people of God.

Dealing with Broken People as Church

What do I do with people who are broken and attend our church? Ministry in today's hurting broken world involves learning to deal effectively with and minister to broken people as church. I'm certain broken and wounded people have always existed in the world and in the family of God. Today, however, we seem to have them in abundance. Unfortunately, many are not attracted to (in fact they are repelled by) the local church. As the church learns to *be* and *do* church in a postmodern and secular world, we have no choice but to answer the pressing question, "What do I do with people who are broken and attend or do not attend our church?" Another way to think about this is, "How do we practice pre- and post-conversion discipleship?"

Broken People in Scripture

Broken people are part of the biblical story and at the heart of the redemptive message of the good news. Christ came to redeem the broken, heal the wounded, and unleash those in bondage and those trapped by baggage from the past. The story of redemption is about taking the broken and redeeming it–making it of value and making it whole. J.I. Packer's excellent book, *Never Beyond Hope: How God Touches and Uses Imperfect People* reviews many such stories of biblical characters. Samson found strength through his weakness (Judg. 14–16). Jacob survived his dysfunctional family (Gen. 25; 27–49). Manoah's wife was barely noticed and not trusted (Judg. 13). Jonah displayed extreme prejudice and great anger at man and God (Jon.). Martha got tangled in misguided priorities (Lk. 10:38–42; Jn. 11:1–44). Thomas just couldn't believe (Jn. 20:19–29); Simon Peter disobeyed, betrayed, and abused (Jn. 21; 1 & 2 Pet.). Noah became drunk and shamed his family (Gen. 9:20–27). Moses was a murderer (Ex. 2:11–15). And the list goes on. God is about making the broken whole. God is about dealing with bondage and baggage. It seems to me if that is what God is about, then that is what the church should be about as we join God in this mission (1 Pet. 2:8–10; Eph. 4; Gen. 11–12).[2]

Attracting Broken People

"Go ye therefore into all the world and as you go reach, teach and baptize…" is the essence of our mission as the people of God (compare Mt. 28:18–20). We are to go into the entire world—as crazy as it is, as broken and wounded as the people are. That is part of our mission. How do we follow the model of Christ and the desire of God for His people in such a broken world? How do we as the people of God attract broken people?

First off, most unchurched broken people are not attracted to the church as a source of healing. In fact, most are repelled by the church and avoid it at all costs. Why? Because for many the church has the reputation as a place and as a people of judgment rather than as a people of grace and healing. The last place a group of broken people want to go is the church.

For instance, David, a young married adult, is seriously searching for God amid a life of misfortune, pain, and spiritual thirsts. Although he is a Bible study leader in his church, he doesn't trust the church or his class enough to share his vulnerabilities and serious questions for fear of being judged. He moves outside his congregation to seek spiritual guidance, encouragement, and spiritual community. What a tragedy for him and the church. The fear he feels of sharing his brokenness is genuine and, unfortunately, probably wise, because most churches refuse to see themselves as hospitals for the broken. They prefer seeing themselves as hotels for the saints.

I heard just today from a pastor who was struggling with two of the church's senior members. They approached him to perform their "wedding" and to bless their relationship and commitment to each other and to God. But they were not planning to get a marriage license and make the marriage legal in the sight of government and society. Their stated reason was because it would stop some of the financial benefits they had as single persons. They didn't want to jeopardize their financial security, so they simply wanted a "blessed union." Now I'm not sure what you hear in this, but I hear some hurting people and a struggling pastor. No one involved wanted the church family to know of the arrangement—for fear of judgment. Now I realize this is a situation packed with many potholes, but the point is that even church members don't bring their hurts and struggles to churches. We hide them and hide behind them because the church is not seen as a place of grace and redemption. Even the pastor was struggling alone at this point. How could he give this faithful couple a "pastoral blessing" on their illegal marriage?

Several years ago a twenty-something unwed mother and father approached me to perform a funeral service for an aborted child. They needed to grieve, and the church wasn't a safe place for them. The child's grandparents needed to grieve, but the church wasn't a safe place for them either. So they quietly approached a friend who was a minister to help them find a way of forgiveness, closure, healing, hope, and redemption. Boy! Seminary didn't prepare me for such a challenge. After much prayer and counsel I agreed. We went through a very, very meaningful worship and healing experience on the banks of the river. God was there in powerful ways. I was able to *be* church for them, and they were able to experience and share God's healing and hope with each other. Could that have happened in a church building? with traditional church people? I wonder.

How do we attract the wounded, hurting, and broken? We must create a safe place for them to fall. We must create an atmosphere of healing and hope rather than judgment and scorn. How? What if we as leaders began to admit to one another how broken we are and began to share our own brokenness, healing, and hurts? What if we let one another know how God is redeeming the wounds of our lives? What if we encouraged and validated the struggle and stories mentioned here by finding a place for such people to share the struggle and the story? What if we helped broken people find a network of folks inside and outside the church who were working with or had moved through similar life passages and pains?

I remember driving my car to a church some time ago. Small and large signs greeted me in the parking lot and in the foyer of the church (which happened to be a theater, not a steepled building). The signs read, "If your world is all together, then you don't belong in this church—we're all broken." Boy! That is permission giving. In worship I heard two powerful and transparent faith stories shared by persons breaking cycles of pain and addiction as sex addicts and alcoholics in recovery. Powerful stories and a powerful sermon and worship experience invited broken people and validated that pain is part of the journey.

What if the church invited and created space for the unchurched and those who "don't have it all together" or are "hidden" to be part of our ministry? What if those hurting who find healing through music were invited into the music ministry? What if those recovering from addictions were invited to apprentice with leaders in small groups and ultimately to lead twelve-step groups? What if those who have been through divorce and maybe remarriage were invited to share their stories, learnings, and healings with those getting married or with couples going through divorce along with their family and friends? Some churches actually have divorce services—similar to wedding services—as a way of healing, validation, and beginning anew. What a great idea!!

What about those living together out of wedlock (a 72 percent increase since the 1990 census according to U.S. Census Bureau statistics) who are parents and desire to participate in a parent-child dedication service? The list goes on and on. The challenges are serious and stretching for the church. How do we open our hearts without compromising our theology? I believe it is possible and vital that we learn.

Practicing Pre-/Post-conversion Discipleship

In the church culture of days gone by, most people had positive feelings about and valued the church and things related to the church. In those days discipleship began, when it happened, after conversion and church membership. Today, with the spiritual thirst rampant in our land and questions about meaning of life around every corner, discipleship is both a pre- and post-conversion challenge. It almost seems like an oxymoron to think of pre-conversion discipleship. But in an age where people are searching and questioning, those opportunities provide excellent entry points for dialogue about belief systems, values, and alignment of head and heart.

A new generation of church members needs a new generation of skills. Our churches must train a core of believers to recognize the opportunities to dialogue with broken people, to be comfortable with skills of theological reflection, to be able to connect the dots of life, aligning heart and head issues. These are skills of pre-conversion discipleship. We can list many other such skills:

1. learning to listen to understand, not to judge
2. learning to discern the timing and presence of the Spirit in a relationship and a situation;
3. learning to assess continuity and discontinuity of issues

4. learning to ask nonthreatening, nonjudgmental questions and to offer biblical concepts and truths at appropriate times
5. learning to help bring meaning and focus to out-of-focus issues for the seeker

These skills are usually practiced in casual trusting relationships outside the traditional church programs. Effective discipleship and sensitivity to others and to the Spirit make such an experience a church experience. When people have a "light bulb moment," an "aha moment," a time "when it all makes sense," God has been present; church has happened.

Such discipleship calls forth a serious and consistent prayer life where believers seek guidance about those to invest in and those to cultivate. Learning to "pay attention" to the Spirit's leading and to see and feel the hurts and heartaches of others prepares the way for discipleship to happen and church to be experienced.

I've watched a young man who was trapped in pain from being raised in a dysfunctional family. He had made bad choices in life when it came to relationships and had felt all the pain he could take. Then he began to move through this type of "unfreezing" of old man and "refreezing" of new man. The journey was long and at times intense. He has told me on more than one occasion, "thanks for sticking with me, for helping me move from a cycle of pain to a cycle of recovery and to find and experience a life of peace I would have never known." The investment in Michael has been significant, but I don't regret it because I've seen an unchurched, spiritually thirsty person find hope, healing, health, and wholeness as he embraces a God-based value system that has led him to a place of peace rather than pain.

Providing a safe place to fall and heal is a critical dimension of spiritual leadership in a broken world. Chuck is a young adult seeking to grow beyond a cycle of bad behaviors and choices in his life. He has worked through painful experiences, false beliefs, and dysfunctional choices learned in his alcoholic family of origin. He accomplished this work because he had a small group and a life coach to listen, to pay attention to him, and to offer him a nonjudgmental place to grow forward. Thus he is developing new beliefs and new behaviors that lead to better decisions and a more peaceful life.

While I was working on this chapter, Randy called to invite me on a conference call with him and Michael (one of his unchurched and skeptical but searching friends) to discuss various views of how people discover and embrace Jesus and God. This person grew up in a highly judgmental family and church. Now he has nothing to do with church. Because he's seen so much change in Randy, he is beginning to ask him what happened to him and how does he experience God. I look forward to this dialogue and will bathe it in much prayer. I will listen and share my journey. As Michael asks, I will point him to scriptural truths. Randy and I are about reframing church for Michael, a hurting and broken life seeking peace and a God he can embrace.

Reframing Church for Broken People

Church has traditionally validated and affirmed the "got it all together" image. We wear our best clothes, our best smile, our best behavior, and our best attitude for those few hours we are in church during the week. The broken and wounded just cannot or will not put on the masks.

What would happen if churches

- provided a "church buddy" for those who visit but know nothing about church? This buddy would offer a warm, nonthreatening relationship to help the person meet others, learn the language, find his or her way around programs and facilities, and answer questions.
- offered life coaches rather than or alongside Sunday school teachers?
- created networks for the broken, wounded, and struggling?
- sponsored small groups for awareness, exploration, or recovery?
- created databases and worked to help those in recovery and those in need—the divorced; the addicted the homosexual, the unwed mother; the codependent; those grief-stricken due to job loss, death, etc.; those abused; or those who abuse?
- provided a safe public forum for persons in the midst of struggle and those in recovery to tell their stories? This could happen in worship, small groups, videos, audio magazines, while serving as worship buddies, etc.
- trained leaders who shared from their journey of brokenness and healing to "walk with" rather than "in front of" and to learn to talk *with* rather than talk *down to* persons in pain?
- affirmed verbally the risks persons take to move from pain to healing and hope?
- lifted up the biblical role models of persons in pain that God used in mission?
- provided a media center stocked with current and effective resources that speak to issues of brokenness and offer an effective psychological, social, faith, and biblical journey out of pain to wholeness?

Such actions and provisions will create an atmosphere of recovery, relationships of trust and integrity, and pathways to health and wholeness. Broken people can't find healthy people—they move in cycles of painful relationships until someone helps them find their way out and learn new skills.

Creating Redemptive Relationships and Structures

Because broken people live in cycles of pain and dysfunction, many are often involved in behaviors, beliefs, and relationships that are not helpful or healing for them. They are often "trapped in a cycle" until new skills are learned and until new relationships of health can be discovered. This shift from unbecoming beliefs, behaviors, and relationships will likely take time. The healthier the person becomes, through the healthy discipling relationship, the more he or she will move away from dysfunction and toward health and wholeness. But it takes time! It's often messy! It will not be perfect!

People finding healthy life paths will experience a "three steps forward and two steps back" pattern while they begin to understand and change old patterns and form new ones. God works in them and through the coaching relationship to new truths. They will discover that good feelings will follow only as they change the old behaviors and bring about new patterns. As they make such changes, they move to recovery and closer to God. During that time believers must

- be church to them
- create the safe place to fall
- help them move toward health and wholeness
- use language they can understand and relate to, while teaching biblical concepts of health, wholeness, and love
- learn to create redemptive structures and relationships to help persons in the meantime, lest they never find full recovery and healing

In the meantime, while wholeness and conversion are in process, safety may become an issue. In these days of sexual predators, fear-based people, and persons motivated by dysfunction and anger, churches need to learn to create a safe place, a place of advocacy and training during times of recovery. So often churches become frightened (which I do understand), and we lock out and shame the ones seeking rebirth and healing because of our own bias and our own fears. Remember "*while* we were yet sinners, Christ died for us" (Rom. 5:8, KJV, emphasis mine). He took the risks for us! Why can't we take the risks for others? Many churches sing "Just as I Am" consistently in worship—now our culture challenges us to live it rather than just sing it.

Mission Baptist Church in a rural community in North Carolina decided to become a disciple-making church. Such a venture has led this sleepy, inward-focused church to become a vibrant community of faith who believe they need to be a safe place for people to fall and to grow in the faith. People actually drive 50+ miles from the "big city" to this church to participate in small groups designed to grow people forward in faith and wholeness.

Myrtle Beach Community Church in the resort area in Myrtle Beach, South Carolina, targets the artistic community. This led them to become a teaching congregation for "Celebrate Recovery" ministry. Their congregation focuses on healing broken and wounded persons who find themselves trapped in dysfunctional relationships or life-altering addictions. God continues to bless this church and ministry as they impact their community for Christ and experience transformation of people and their community.

Coaching Questions for Leaders and Congregations

- What are the issues in this chapter that are calling for your attention?
- How could you prioritize these issues to make them manageable and not overwhelming for you and your congregation?
- What resources does your church already have for dealing with broken people?
- Who are the advocates for these issues that you might dialogue and pray with to discern next steps?
- Who are you willing to contact and dialogue with?
- When will you do this?
- What will you then need to do with this information to help move the congregation forward in faith and function?

Performing Exegesis on Culture So You Can Share the Good News

I taught children during the early part of my ministry. They taught me many valuable lessons. One valuable lesson was that until I understood their world I could not clearly communicate new truths, develop deeper trust, or find meaning in my relationship with them and theirs with me. When I understood something of their human development and where they were in family life and what their learning styles and capabilities were, I could connect with them in a meaningful learning environment. When I learned that they, too, were teaching me and that we could learn together about this world we were in, we experienced a bond and community that became meaningful for each of us. Such trust helped move us deeper and deeper in appreciation of each other. We developed new understanding together as we were experiencing our vast world. You might say that until I could perform exegesis on their culture I could not effectively share life's lessons. The teacher has not really taught until the student really learns.

Such life lessons in my early career experiences continued to hold true as I shifted from working with children to working with adults. Adults learn when we have to learn. Learning to seek and use the teachable moments in the lives of various generations of adults became a stack pole for my ministry of Christian education. Whether they were single parent families, blended families, dysfunctional families, adults in dual career marriages, single adults, financially distressed adults, adults trapped in addictions, etc., all became part of me learning to read the culture of the adult so we could frame an avenue for sharing the good news. Leonard Sweet explains, "Learning to read the culture is like that of a semiotician." That is learning to read the "signs of the times and culture" demands that we distinguish what we do as disciples of Jesus from others who are "reading the signs." It all begins with hearing and listening, then receiving the true voices that are out there, the voices of the Spirit, not just the culture. "We need to be in touch with the culture but in tune with the Spirit."[3] Learning to perform exegesis on the culture of churched adults was a challenge within itself with the diversity of needs that were emerging.

Now I'm having to learn to perform exegesis on the unchurched culture that I have been basically oblivious to because I've been so consumed by my church culture. I've had to make some life changes and spiritual commitments in order to learn something of the needs, teachable moments, and life challenges of unchurched adults. Giving a percentage of my time to this venture has awakened me spiritually and professionally like nothing else I've ever done. I've learned something about tithing my time, money, and knowledge base within the unchurched community.

Trying to find and network with the spiritually thirsty, unchurched adults is now part of my daily personal ministry. My professional ministry is trying to take these learnings into my church venues. I've been intentionally connecting with the spiritually thirsty, unchurched community for the last fourteen years. My book *Reframing Spiritual Formation* explains something of the shifts I have had to wrestle with as a Christian educator in an unchurched world. This book is an attempt to share some of the ways I've learned to build bridges with the unchurched of the postmodern world rather than erecting the barriers many of them feel church people are proficient at building.

Brian McLaren encountered much of the same epiphany. He explains: "My linear Liar-Lunatic-or-Lord arguments, either-or propositions, and watertight belief system didn't enhance the credibility of the gospel for my new friend; rather, they made the gospel seem less credible, maybe even a little cheap and shallow." Brian further declares, "the way we traditionally expressed Christianity may be in trouble, but the future may hold new expressions of Christian faith every bit as effective, faithful, meaningful, and world-transforming as those we have known before."[4] The hints of this newness continue to challenge me to learn to understand this culture and find ways of sharing the good news in it.

Learning to Read the Signs in a Secular Culture

Performing exegesis on the culture means simply trying to understand the signs, symbols, and meanings inherent in the culture's practices, behaviors, rituals, relationships, etc. The prophets of old were interested in "reading the signs," and the New Testament is filled with stories of looking for and following signs. What are the signs the church of today needs to pay attention to in order to see, hear, and follow God's movement in our world?

A recent discovery for me was something in the Christmas narrative, which I have heard and read for years. A spiritually thirsty, unchurched person helped me to see that the wise men didn't have access to the Scriptures to find Jesus. They saw a sign in that which they knew and encountered regularly—the stars. These wise men saw the star—before they saw Jesus. They would likely have not found Jesus if they had not first seen the star. Most stars are best seen when in the dark. The unchurched person found great meaning for this truth of learning to find God through the familiar and of finding meaning for the dark and challenging times in life. When this *eureka* was shared, I was able to read the signs and inquired carefully:

- What are the places/experiences you encounter regularly that may be pointing you to truth?
- What light and greater truth than you've known is your star pointing to beyond your darkness?
- How is the star leading you beyond where you are to where you desire to be?

These questions opened up a dialogue among the unchurched, spiritually thirsty, which created an "aha" for several of us during the Christmas season. This helped me begin to see the value of learning to "read the signs." Reading the signs among church people usually revolves around prayer, worship attendance, Bible study interest or involvement, devotional life, etc. Reading the signs among the unchurched who are spiritually thirsty involves discernment of where God might be moving them from a "life pinch" to a "life eureka or truth." Discerning the signs might lead us to pay closer attention to

- music they listen to and find meaning in
- language they use, identify with, and respond to
- media they pay attention to and embrace
- books, magazines, Web sites they frequent in their search for truth and help for life pinches
- places they frequent that seem to offer a respite and sanctuary for them

The tough thing for me was that I often tried to impose my church values on them while ignoring things they were connected with as meaningful experiences that could serve as a pathway in their spiritual journey. I also wanted them to "convert" to my God, my church, my belief system sooner than later. I quickly discovered among many postmoderns that they had a much stronger need to belong before they pursued belief or shift in behaviors. This was quite a shift in my tradition and training. Reading the culture takes time, intentionality, prayer, reflection, and dialogue. Bill Easum, Tom Bandy, and others have framed this shift, which reflects a deep reading of the signs of our times.

Church Culture Values	Postmodern Culture Values
Believe (like us)	Belong (among us)
Behave (like us)	Behave (shifts toward health)
Belong (with us)	Believe (confirmed by shifts)

Notice the sequence in each column. These appear to be progressive values. Church culture focused and focuses on doctrinal issues as avenue for membership. People who join us must believe like us, behave like us, and *then* we will consider them as belonging. (Now to be honest—it's one thing to join many churches and quite another thing for those who join to really feel as if they belong. Many join but still feel like outsiders for a long time because they were not born in the "right community" to the "right family" or in the "right part of the country.")

Postmoderns, on the other hand, want to belong first. They want to be trusted, respected as individuals on a journey that is often unique and different from the "norm" of most in the church culture. Once they experience belonging, they move into making some adjustments in behavior and beliefs. They make such adjustments not to fit in with the church culture as much as because of the greater faith and wholeness they discover and grow into while experiencing and benefiting from belonging to the community.

Discerning Truth Amid Differences of Values/Preferences

How then do you discern authenticity, genuineness, and intentional movement toward God and truth amidst differences of values, preferences, and traditions? That is the $64,000 question for many. Let me share some things I have learned while seeking to communicate the good news with integrity to persons who have a spiritual interest but are not necessarily attracted to church as I've known it.

Let me set the context. I am deeply investing my time, skills, and money in about ten spiritually thirsty, unchurched persons. More peripherally, I deal fairly consistently with about thirty others who are in some way connected to the core ten. Most are under 40—many under 30—and most are professional. Some are single, some married with children. These folks are scattered all across the country. About half would be considered in the upper economic bracket. All have a serious thirst for meaning, and most are working to understand who they are, where they are headed, and how to untangle some of the painful experiences of the past or present. They seek to learn to live a life that is whole and healed.

Through the years I'm learning lessons and indicators that validate for me the seriousness and forward movement of most of these in a spiritual journey toward truth, wholeness, and God. Among those lessons are the following:

- Open-ended questions provide a forum for dialogue.
- Judgmental attitude or directives close down the conversation.
- Consistency of communication builds trust and creates openness.
- Scripture is taught through natural interactions at appropriate times and places where divine truths can help illuminate meaning in human situations and personal life pinches.
- Listening with heart, head, spirit, and ears is critical but hard work.
- Learning to focus and pay attention to their world, their concerns, their heartaches, their questions, their relationships, and their

search is more important than my agenda or my need to "share my faith."

- Earning the right to be heard and the right to share my faith story takes time and energy and depends on divine timing.
- Church language is often a barrier to facilitating the uncovering of Truth and to introducing someone to a deeper and more meaningful spiritual walk.
- Learning to recognize teachable moments and divine appointments creates opportunity for sharing and connecting biblical truths to human pinches.
- Prayer is about listening to the Spirit's leading in these relationships and provides an avenue for walking with hurting people in their struggles.
- Community is the place of hope, healing, and redemption for many of these people.
- Community is about belonging and having a safe place rather than having a teacher, preacher, and text.
- Worship is experienced over and over as "aha's come" when divine truths connect to human stories and as new truths are discovered and new behaviors are shaped.
- Sharing of life on life and gifts on gifts is the essence of these relationships and of a shared spiritual journey.

Indicators that suggest authenticity and genuineness of their spiritual journey include the following:

- Openness to dialogue about faith issues, meaning of life, life pinches, and relationship struggles
- Curiosity about spiritual things, meaning of life, and pursuit of truth
- Needing to discover meaning in life's challenges, pains, and struggles
- Working to connect head and heart
- Wanting to break old cycles of behavior and attitudes that have proven destructive
- Wanting to find ways of redeeming life
- Desire to find their place in the world and to work and live out of their passions and callings
- Knowing there's more than they have known or experienced
- Openness to prayer—listening to and talking with "higher powers"
- Desire to "connect with the energy and design of the universe"
- Willingness to take a moral inventory and to explore consequences of choices they have made

- Openness to learning to articulate their existing belief system, to finding the gaps in it, and to beginning to rethink it to help with life transformation
- Ability to move from selfish to selfless in thinking and behavior
- Desire to leave unhealthy for healthy
- Desire to move forward toward greater health, happiness, wholeness, and maturity

Pathways to the Good News for a Postmodern World

Beyond the indicators and lessons, I've noted what are proving to be legitimate and fruit-bearing pathways to sharing the good news in a postmodern world. I am not suggesting these are foolproof or complete. I am suggesting that these seem to be what and where I sense God moving in the relationships I've already discussed. Brian McLaren suggests that "there are three themes—'rivers' that seem to be shaping the contours of ministry in a post-modern age—spiritual transformation, authentic community, and missional current."[5]

Some might say this is the coach approach to evangelism and discipleship. This approach forces you to ask serious questions:

- What are you learning about ministry in a postmodern world?
- What is God using in your world as you seek to communicate the good news to persons outside the church and beyond many of our long-standing church traditions?
- What are the questions that help self-assessment, self-direction, self-correction, and life transformation?
- How can we help uncover the movement of the Spirit in someone's life and empower them to connect with the Spirit and the reason for which they were created?

New Frames for Old Truths

I recently decided to reframe some pictures I've had for some time. I really liked the pictures, but they just didn't fit in with the décor in my new home. I looked and looked to replace the pictures, but couldn't find anything I liked. Someone suggested reframing the existing pictures. It worked. I got to keep what I embraced and the re-matting and reframing helped make it more enjoyable and functional in my new home. It seems that is what's happening with my framework for ministry in this rapidly changing age.

Language is a critical piece of the spiritual journey. So many postmoderns can't or will not embrace church language. Some carry bad baggage from bad church experiences in their past. Others simply have no frame of reference by which to understand or value this language to define their journeys. In similar fashion the church culture has great difficulty in valuing the language introduced here as a way of explaining their spiritual journey.

The following list represents language and concepts that seem to be emerging for me and that are adding value to ministry with postmodern persons searching for truth.

Holy ears

I'd never thought about or heard the term "Holy Ears" until about three years ago. One of my postmodern friends called and asked me to sit in on a conversation with them and some of their friends and to be their "Holy Ears." I was invited only to listen and then to share with them what I had heard as they sought earnestly to connect their life experiences with their emerging belief system. They wanted me to help them connect biblical truths to their life pinches and circumstances.

Disconnect

This term seems to help us when we are working with concepts of "missing the mark," "sin," or "disobedience" from a modern church world vocabulary. "Disconnect" indicates where one part of life "disconnects" with head or heart. Disconnect represents the situation where an alignment is called for between what one is living, thinking, and feeling and what one is learning needs to happen to move them forward in health and wholeness.

Connecting with the Universe

This concept was a little scary to me at first. I thought this indicated a New Age philosophy or syncretism of beliefs. When I listened and sought to understand clearly—rather than imposing my beliefs before understanding—I discovered connecting with the universe is a serious thing. It represents a deep desire to align one's life to the reason they were created. The challenge and desire are to live into their destiny. The universe has personal qualities and intended virtues God implants from the beginning.

Connecting Head and Heart

This is the clearest language I've found for conversion, for shifting of values, for a balanced lifestyle, and for an intent to live out of who God created us to be. Helping the unchurched find language that clearly and accurately portrays their journey is important to nurturing their spiritual journey. Learning to listen and not judge is critical. So is building a trust base so heart can be shared. Heart must be modeled through our transparency, vulnerability, and shared journey of faith formation. Filled with struggles, such a journey leads to celebrations of connecting with our calling, our created purpose, and our Creator.

Life Coach

These fellow journeyers I'm walking with call me their life coach. I'd never thought about this before, but that is the way they describe me and introduce me these days. I add value to their lives through the questions I ask, the listening I engage with them in, and the pursuit of truth we share. I really do function as a spiritual friend and guide and pastor in their journey. I'm not the only guide, friend, or pastor among the group; but I am looked to by most as a lead life coach.

Connecting with Others on a Similar Journey

This is akin to discipleship and evangelism in the church culture. Finding and connecting with those on a similar journey is fun and fulfilling. The group also becomes a group to celebrate and grow with and from. Community is vital.

Experiencing Community or Building a Surrogate Family

This represents a crying need in our transient culture filled with persons who, for the most part, grew up in broken and dysfunctional family systems. Finding and experiencing authentic community is about building a surrogate family system of trusting and trustworthy relationships with persons who share similar value systems and interests. Ethan Watters's sociological study, *Urban Tribes: A Generation Redefines Friendship, Family and Commitment*[6] is a great look at this trend in the postmodern age. Robert Putnam's *Better Together*[7] adds significant insights to this sociological phenomenon that is and will continue to impact spiritual life formation and church in a postmodern world.

Unfreezing/Refreezing

These terms seem to offer concepts the church crowd captures in "old man," "new man," and "conversion." Unfreezing helps the unchurched understand a need to change what has proven to be destructive in their pursuit of truth and wholeness. Refreezing means to learn new behaviors, attitudes, values, and beliefs through exploration with community and reflection on Scripture then. The unchurched want to refreeze those new concepts, beliefs, values, and behaviors that help them move forward in their journey as they learn to live into their destiny and God-created purpose.

Being "Graced Today"

Several of my fellow journeyers have used this term to celebrate and explain an epiphany, a conversion, a new reality that works as they connect heart and head with God's intention. When the alignment and embracing of new truths are experienced and the new satisfaction of being obedient comes, it proves to be very empowering. The Spirit is felt, and "power is given to do greater things." They understand they don't deserve the grace or the experience, but they are profoundly grateful for the journey and the community that helped them find and experience "being graced."

Alignment of Life

This term is often used when heart and head connect, when new beliefs are embraced and expressed in ways that bring hope, healing, and relief from pain and struggle. Alignment of life refers to movement toward the "new creation" as they watch all "old things pass away."

Fine-tuning

This term is used when newness occurs but the person still needs Biblical understanding and a language to connect experience with new beliefs and values. Fine-tuning is a great image. When this alignment happens, the sound of life is clearer and more pleasing.

Inner Peace instead of Struggle

This indicates an embracing of the new beliefs, values, and behaviors. The new heart is growing stronger. God is making Himself known, and celebration and gratitude emerge as genuine and deep qualities of life.

Redemptive Acts/Relationships

This term describes how you can move forward from painful relationships and experiences to experience relief, hope, healing, health, and wholeness. This process guides the pilgrim toward understanding and value of redemption. The process involves beginning with something that is worthless and often painful. Because of new beliefs and of connection to God's design and intent, newness emerges. Then personal transformation of heart and head are celebrated.

These are several of those challenges and learning curves I've encountered over the years. I am keenly aware that some of this will cause some readers discomfort because I am moving away from traditionally accepted church or biblical language. My review of church history helps me to see that language and leadership roles have shifted throughout Christian history. I suspect it is shifting again.

Coaching Questions to Consider

1. What can you affirm in this chapter?
2. What challenges would you offer to my thoughts on finding Christ in our culture?
3. How might you make some life and ministry adjustments that will align you to those things you can affirm?
4. What challenging issues might you want to explore further?
5. Who could help you explore these issues?
6. What is your next step?

5

The Medium

Moving from Wandering to Walking

Leadership Challenges

"We just need a vision and a leader. Our pastor seems afraid of casting a vision and leading our people, therefore we are just drifting and spinning our wheels as a congregation."

"How can I lead without becoming a domineering dictator? I want to lead people who think and who own a vision that is theirs and not just mine."

"How can I lead when those I am called to lead do not want to change?"

"If we only had a leader, we could move forward as a church."

How many times have I heard these statements from frustrated clergy and lay leaders during my years of consultation and coaching! Everyone seems to be looking for someone to blame! Few take ownership of the issue and change themselves even if they can't change the group or other person.

Today's church faces a clear and fairly pervasive void of leadership. The reasons for this are manifold. The leaders' training is now obsolete for their context. Leaders have received little or no training. Most often leaders avoid the leadership role to appease the comforts of the membership or because they fear being perceived as dictators.

So often leadership is filled with challenges that most clergy are not gifted for or called into. Leaders face the challenge of the culture and of maintaining integrity with the gospel mandates. Research has proven time after time that most clergy are gifted to care and nurture rather than to administrate and lead.[1] Until very recent years leadership has not been a core class in most seminaries.

Seminaries have taught clergy to be good at "pastoral care" and "expository preaching," and to be theologically correct. Such has generated a growing number of congregations who expect their clergy to be good in the pulpit and in the crisis or nurturing situation rather than to lead into the future. When the few clergy who are leaders are matched with congregations who are more concerned about "caring for us" rather than "reaching them," the congregation and the leader are frustrated.

Such represents the difference between spiritual leadership *in* the church and the focus of this section, spiritual leadership *through* the church. Spiritual leadership *in* the church sees their primary function as preserving the institution and its history. Often these leaders give verbal assent to carrying out the biblical mission, but their behavior and schedule more often than not are dominated by institutional concerns over mission objectives. Spiritual leadership *through* the church focuses more on mobilizing members for mission rather than pacifying members or maintaining institutional matters. Spiritual leadership *as* the church dissolves the distinctions between clergy and laity and creates a mission-minded, culture-penetrating partnership for the cause of Christ.

While I was working with a pastor of an old downtown First Baptist Church, the pastor came to the coaching session weary of "fighting with naysayers" in his congregation who were opposing suggested change. These were loyalists to the institution's history and heritage and not really concerned about its mission. Through the coaching session he was able to accept this reality and arrive at a plan he was willing to embrace. The plan was designed to reduce his struggle with this group and to move forward with those who wanted to move forward. He realized he was giving the naysayers so much time and energy that he was enabling their behaviors. This drained his energy for birthing the new. Such a "eureka" for him caused an internal shift. This shift changed schedule, energy flow, and meeting agendas. It surfaced boundaries he put in place to rebuild his motivation for birthing the new while minimizing the time he gave to those who were just maintenance-minded. He began to serve the mission and not just the people. I heard from him again while writing this chapter. He was celebrating that "the church is turning another corner. The mission-minded are stepping up to the plate and joining hands so the church can go on mission and stop fighting institutional battles." Wow!! Aha!!

Being a Leader without Becoming a Dictator

To move our churches effectively into the twenty-first century our church leaders must become more intentional in leadership. Often even good and godly leaders get lost in the leadership maze, or weary from the leadership challenges. Have you ever felt like you were living a fast-paced life but were getting nowhere fast? Have you ever served in various capacities in church life, spending night after night and day after day involved in choirs, committees, teams, and activities, but suddenly realized you had lost evidence of God's movement and leadership in your life? What about looking at all the financial, human, and building resources your church possesses? Ask, what are we tangibly contributing to the kingdom of God through all our activities, investments, contributions, and facilities? I've been in these positions and asked these questions, and I've encountered many others who seem to struggle with similar issues. Let me suggest that we follow the counsel of Moses and Joshua as they moved the people of God from "wandering" (Exodus and Deuteronomy) to "walking" (Josh. 1).

Making an Accurate Assessment

Ask yourself honestly the following questions and discuss your responses with other leaders.

1. What consumes most of my time and discussion in church committee or team meetings?
2. How can I become a more intentional church leader and lead our congregation to pursue vital ministry and join God in His mission in the world?
3. What are the front burner issues that get prime time in announcements, sermons, Bible study lessons, or discipleship courses?

4. What percentage of my time and energy go to pacifying those in the pews rather than nurturing those who desire to birth the future?

When I talk with churches and leaders about these issues, the same issues repeatedly dominate the discussion. These include caregiving, praying for the sick/bereaved, concerns about world issues related to war, building and program maintenance and development, fund raising, and budget concerns. While these are important issues, most of them are focused primarily on us–the membership–and not on reaching or ministering to the hurting, broken world of which we are apart. If 70 to 80 percent of your time, energy, and resources go to these issues, your church is likely in a maintenance or survival mode. You are wandering aimlessly when it comes to being on God's mission in the world. Let me encourage you to consider moving from wandering in the wilderness of self-care and institutional preservation to mission–walking with God into His mission in the church and through the church in the world. Shift your committee, team, or Bible studies and sermons from "us" to "them." *The mission of the New Testament church is more about God's mission to the hurting, broken, lame, and lost than about institutional maintenance or pastoral care; but many church leaders have lost sight of this Great Commission and Great Commandment.*

Moving from Wandering to Walking— Becoming an Intentional Leader

More often than not our committee agendas, team priorities, budget allocations, and church programming have more to do with keeping up with the flock and keeping us satisfied and happy than with impacting our culture, reaching the unreached, and learning to *be* salt, light and leaven in a broken, hurting world. Such comes from the values, personal preferences, and local traditions of the core leaders of the congregation. Could these self-serving values and preferences be responsible for approximately 80 percent of the churches in our country being classified as plateaued or dying?[2]

How can our leadership shift this detrimental value system and realign our preferences with Kingdom values, Kingdom priorities, and Godly virtues that will fulfill the Great Commission and the Great Commandment and impact our world for the cause of Christ? Let me make a few suggestions and challenge you to make yours to your leadership core.

First and foremost, we must be *called back to the biblical mission and mandate for the Church.* Far too often we do church based on our preferences and not on God's mandates and instructions.

- Restudy the founding of the New Testament church in the Book of Acts.
- Review the essence of what it means to be the people of God through a serious study of Ephesians.
- Use the Books of Timothy, Titus, Acts, and Ephesians to assess and realign what it means to be a church leader. (For a survey of the New Testament's perspective on leadership, visit www.transformingsolutions.org.)
- Study the New Testament to rediscover what a disciple of Christ looks like, how a disciple of Christ behaves, and how a disciple is to function in the world and the church.

Next, I would suggest that leaders become *intentional in their prayer life*. Our faith activates God's power. Learning to pray is a vital part of a disciple's lifestyle and the source of a disciple's energy, guidance, direction, and power. We seek to lead far too often without the presence, leadership, and empowerment that come only through our connection with God.

If you're like me, the first two issues are not likely to happen consistently unless we *submit ourselves to accountability relationships.* Invite a trusted person or group of persons to hold you accountable for study, review, prayer, and an honest assessment. Accountability is not about imposing something on you. Rather, accountability is about helping you to stay focused and moving forward toward goals you set for yourself. I've been in accountability relationships since seminary. In fact, these relationships are probably the greatest gift and most enduring aspect of my seminary education. We are scattered across the country, but we communicate regularly via e-mail, phone, and planned face-to-face play and work times. We invite each other to ask key questions designed to keep us moving forward in faith and function toward Kingdom goals. Today Christian coaching relationships offer me and countless others this dimension of leadership development and accountability.

Finally, let me suggest that you *intentionally change the way you approach your leadership roles and functions in church life.* Rather than simply going with the flow, invite accountability partners to help you find balance. Here are some suggestions that have been helpful in my journey.

- **Seek balance in prayer and care and giving**. Spend as much time, energy, and money on reaching those outside the fellowship as you spend on those inside the congregation.

- **Share your concerns and burdens for others inside and outside the church walls** in public prayer times.
- **Lead the congregation to learn about and respond to** community and world issues—poverty; spouse abuse; homelessness; injustice in the systems of government, school, etc.; unwed mothers; AIDS; family concerns; and financial mismanagement.
- **Call out the called** during your worship and small group ministry. Make sure that your congregation knows they have permission, encouragement, and support for following God's call on their life to touch the hurts of the world.
- **Invite community leaders to partner with you in ministry projects.** Tutors are needed in schools. Partnerships are needed with county agents, social service agencies, and United Way. Other denominations and other churches in your community can partner and make significant impact on the hurts of your community. A growing number of churches are creating very energizing partnerships that are energizing their congregations toward growth and greater faithfulness and effectiveness.
- **Validate and commission volunteers** who are members of your congregation who volunteer in the hospitals, agencies, military, Red Cross, Disaster Relief, etc.
- **Learn to resource and support those believers in their ministry in the work-a-day world.** Countless numbers of Christian are in what Jesus called the "fields that are white unto harvest" as they teach in our public schools, care in our hospital systems, lead in our government agencies, etc. How can your church validate this ministry and activate ministry in the world?[3]

Moving from wandering to intentional walking into the new requires faith, courage, and willingness to live with some degree of the unknown. God calls us "to walk by faith and not by sight." Start walking into intentional discipleship. Spiritual leadership in a secular age challenges leaders to learn to engage in pre- and post-conversion discipleship. Learning to meet the spiritually thirsty where they are in their faith journey calls for new skills and commitments.[4]

Leadership is not about becoming a dictator but about becoming a faithful disciple. Leadership is about living into your calling, gifting, and the mission of the church. Leadership is about finding those people of passion that God wants to move forward in their faith and function, and serving with gifts God provides you and the group. Sometimes others can move into their mission without the gifts of leadership you provide to the community of faith. But when a leader steps forward to lead, the army of spectators in our churches becomes an army on mission in the Kingdom! The blending of the gifts of the saints propels the mission forward.

Leadership Designations in the New Testament

Leadership in the New Testament has many facets and faces. Libraries of books have been written about the biblical framework of leadership, so I'm not going to repeat that here. I want to draw out some implications of leadership for a secular age. John Stott unveils a clear and significant distinction in his book, *Christian Mission in the Modern World: What the Church Should Be Doing NOW!* Stott declares, "Moreover, in working towards this goal God uses 'men and women both inside and outside the churches,' and the church's particular role in the mission of God is to 'point to God at work in world history,' to discover what he is doing, to catch up with it and to get involved in it ourselves. For God's primary relationship is to the world, it was argued, so that the true sequence is to be found no longer in the formula 'God-church-world' but in the formula 'God-world-church.' This being so, it is the world that must be allowed to provide the agenda for the churches'—the churches taking the world seriously and seeking to serve according to its contemporary sociological needs."[5]

Servant Leaders in a Secular Age

How can a church begin to assess leadership effectiveness of the paid and volunteer staff of their church? How can needed alignments or adjustments be made without exploding the congregation? These are questions this section will guide you through.

Biblical teachings help us see clearly that servant leadership is a chief ingredient of spiritual leadership in a pagan, post-Christian world. What does servant leadership look like in a secular age? How can clergy and lay leaders lead without becoming or being perceived as dictators? Such a review of the biblical framework for church leaders allows congregations to do a reality check. Where are we aligned with scriptural guidelines? What are the places we need to work on to be more biblically accurate?

All too often church leadership structures and roles take on personalities of leaders or preferences of groups or families without much regard for biblical guidelines. The role of deacon and elder is one place this often happens. Their roles often follow tradition, personal preferences of a few, or the misguided expectations of the congregation without much regard for the biblical framework. After reviewing this survey, ask yourself these coaching questions:

- What are the biblical principles of leadership you work from easily and consistently?
- What are the biblical concepts of leadership you find most difficult to embrace and to make a part of yourself?
- Who is your primary role model for leadership?
- What are the adjustments God is calling for that will make you a stronger leader and more pleasing to Him?
- What do you need to live into these new realities?
- Who can help you?
- *What are you willing to do and by when?*

Deacon (Servant Leaders)

Deacons form an integral part of the leadership team for the New Testament church. Having served as a deacon consultant, I'm increasingly reminded how much leadership deacons actually have in local churches. Regardless of the model of ministry a local church decides to use to frame their ministry, deacons lead the church. In whatever direction the deacons lead the church, you can expect the church to go there. This can be good! This can also be catastrophic for the church. I'm convinced that a local church will never go beyond its spiritual leadership. Depending on the church preference and expectations, I've seen deacons function as spiritual leaders *in, through,* and/or *as* the church. The church value system, culture, and expectations seem to frame the form and function of a church's deacon ministry rather than the New Testament. Review what the New Testament says about deacons. Such a review can once again serve as a reality check for you as a leader and the body of deacons in your church.

The pastor of a small congregation in what was becoming a high growth area is facing "the charter members and old guard of the church." They believe their deacons are to be their care-givers rather than servant models in the church. The pastor had been talking about this reality and leading the church leaders to explore this for about three years. He called me to say, "I think we're now ready to explore some different models of deacon ministry that might help us be a more effective church amidst a growing community." We talked for some time, affirming his patience with change and summarizing several models. Following the call he was excited, motivated, and had a plan to take back to his core group seeking to find and take next steps. Sometimes it's not that churches are stuck by choice. They just don't see other options. Exploring options opens new doors of potential and leadership. A review of the biblical roles of deacon opened up some new realities this church had not see before.

When this congregation reviewed these New Testament guidelines for deacons and other concepts, they understood that their current membership was not on the same page on issues like women deacons and the role of elders versus deacons. They did come to realize that as they grow and reach out to their new community they are likely to find more diversity of opinions and beliefs. Consequently, they decided to do some further study of these issues, including some surveys among newcomers and prospects from the community to help them determine discrepancies and potential issues they may face in the future. The function of their deacons and leadership here became very clear. They were catalysts for change, for exploring new frontiers of ministry, and for educating the congregation about biblical realities and a shifting community context and culture.

A quick review of Scriptures related to church leadership roles leads me to believe that function is much more important than form in the New Testament. We discover that leadership roles, more often than not, are greatly influenced by the historical nature of the church in a specific culture. History and culture lay behind the shifts the church has made in its vision of itself and in its expectations of its leaders. Leaders always face new realities and new shifts. Leaders are called upon to move organizations, communities, and churches through the shifts. The distinction about spiritual leadership is how do we face cultural shifts and personal preference shifts without jeopardizing the biblical mandates and mission of the people of God?

Leadership Realities in a Secular Age

Leading congregations or faith communities in a postmodern and post-Christian world offers many challenges. It's great to know that these are not new or insurmountable challenges for Christian leaders. Such challenges and shifts were encountered by Paul and have been summarized by Gene Wilkes. Wilkes explains, "Paul wrestled with major shifts in how he related to God, his thinking about God, and how he did ministry."

Shift 1: From Law to Grace. How he perceived the way to salvation (Gal. 2:8–9)

Shift 2: From Jews to Gentiles, from his people to other people as his primary target group; from places where he was most comfortable to places where he was uncomfortable (Acts 13:44–46; Eph. 3:6)

Shift 3: From Professional Clergy to Gifted and Called Layperson as primary persons who should lead among God's people (Acts 14:23; Titus 1:5)

Shift 4: From Centralized Church to Decentralized Church (Acts 17:17) as the core strategy; from waiting for people to come to the local place of worship to setting up shop in the marketplace (Acts 5:42; 20:20)

Shift 5: From Church Base to World Focus (Acts 1:8; 28:30–31) as the base of operations; from the temple in Jerusalem to house churches planted among the various groups he sought to reach for Christ

Shift 6: From His People to All People as ministry focus (Eph. 2:14–16; Gal. 3:27–29); from reaching and serving one nation, the Jews, to reaching and leading all people who confess that Jesus is Lord[6]

Wilkes's overview of the shifts in Paul's ministry give clear indication that leadership effectiveness calls forth growth and shifts in the leaders' understanding of who you are, who God is, how God acts, and of where God is leading. Spiritual leadership *through* the church is about discerning the movement of God in and through the people of God—the body of Christ. Leadership is not about being a dictator who calls the shots but about being a leader who empowers and leads people to discern and follow God into their world.

Being a leader without becoming a dictator is about

- pulling, not pushing people
- asking and empowering rather than telling
- listening first and talking later
- building teams and communities rather than building buildings
- empowering laypersons for ministry rather than enlisting them in program maintenance
- inclusiveness rather than exclusiveness
- finding next steps rather than arriving at a destination
- discernment rather than declaring
- contextualizing ministry rather than demanding conformity
- creativity rather than conformity
- creating nonthreatening entry points that build community
- connecting the dots of life rather than connecting with church programs
- discovering language that communicates truths rather than preserving language that is comfortable

After reviewing the shifts Paul encountered in his shifting culture, what shifts do you see that you or your congregation may be facing in order to move your ministry forward? We cannot change anything that we do not acknowledge. Let me encourage you to take a close and honest inventory of your leadership style and of the value system that guides the way you do and experience church. Are you more into being a dictator to preserve your preferences or to work within your comfort zones? Or are you interested in being a servant who guides and leads into lands you might not know?

Let me encourage you to think of leadership as a significant function in the body of Christ and to assess the function and balance of that leadership in your church. Far too often we feel leadership is about preserving forms rather than leading missions.

Determining the Form and Function of Leadership in Your Church

Every organization and family system has leaders that emerge or are appointed. A review of New Testament passages related to leadership forms and functions seems to suggest that the New Testament is much more concerned about the *function* of leaders than the *form* or structures they work through. I see this lived out in many congregations where the "rules of the church" are set by the personal beliefs and preferences of a matriarch or patriarch and/or their family members. It is often assumed that a deep investment financially or otherwise that a person or family makes to the church should earn them the right to dictate the agenda of the church, even though such assumptions go against biblical teaching. Such assumptions generate great heartache for many and total apathy in others. They often create barriers to reaching the unchurched world.

The New Testament seems to suggest that the leader's life, character, and abilities are part of one's divine gifting and calling. The New Testament assumes that the church will affirm and acknowledge such gifting and calling. Leadership is not about "lording over someone or dominating them" as much as it is about taking steps ahead of them, walking with them, and leading them through discernment of the movement of God in and around the body of Christ. Leadership involves calling, gifting, personality traits, and spiritual formation and function in the body of Christ. What are some ideas for discerning the movement of God *through* the church? What are some tools leaders might use to assist in gaining clarity of reality and next steps?

An illustration of this comes from the pastor of the historic downtown First Baptist Church I referred to earlier. The pastor's "aha" came when he understood he could not transform the church until he transformed himself. The reinventing of an organization begins with the reinventing of leaders as they seek the face and leadership of

God. The threat and fears associated with reinventing lie heavy on the thresholds of many leaders and prevent them from moving forward and moving the organization they lead forward.

Just today, I got a phone call from a person on our convention staff wanting some help with their team. She indicated they needed a vision and purpose statement for the staff that would lead them to fulfill the organization's mission. The more we talked the more fear and discomfort I detected. She, like so many of us, fears changing who she is to become a different leader. What can you do differently that will help ensure a more effective leadership function?

See appendix 2 for a leadership readiness inventory compiled for congregations and pastors/staff who are seeking to find and take their next steps in a spiritual strategic journey. This tool should assist you and your congregation in finding and taking some next steps in your growth journey. For more information about this coach approach to congregational development visit the suggested Web sites.[7]

Moving from Maintenance to Mission: Revisiting the Purpose of the Church

Some leaders and congregations who are still concerned about leadership *in* the church may choose to deny discovered or suspected realities and do nothing at this point. While leaders are key, how churches see and embrace their mission is just as critical if not more so. Many times revisioning begins with exploring biblical mandates for the church, needs assessment, community demographics, and exploration of strengths and weaknesses. From there adjustments are made: new teams formed, new mission statements developed, new goals and strategies crafted. As you take more intentional steps in leading the congregation forward, let me encourage you to review the biblical mandate for the church.

I would like to suggest that you begin with a core group of leaders who are people of passion, not necessarily people of position, and help them do the following:

- Revisit biblical mandates for the church and individual believers.
- Discover their call as believers. (Often the call is that place where the world's greatest needs intersect with a person's passions). The group can also discern their spiritual giftedness (Scripture indicates that every believer has at least one spiritual gift that is given to equip us for ministry), and claim and engage in a personal ministry;[8] (your personal ministry is that thing that God has created you to be engaged with and that allows you to exercise

your role in the mission of the church as part of the body of Christ).

- Create a permission-giving atmosphere (an environment that nurtures the birthing of the new rather than just clinging to what we have experienced in the past; not an environment of control but of empowerment) in which these discoveries can be acted on, thus creating new energies and indicators of God's movement in the midst of the church that the masses can observe.[9]
- Encourage and coach the "called out" to share stories of God's movement and their discoveries in their journey with their families, small groups, and the larger congregation.

Revisiting biblical concepts around leadership and the mission of the church provides excellent framework for unleashing the church in the secular world as the people of God discover and embrace their call, giftedness, and personal ministry. The above pattern will provide a new record of the business of the church and a trained core for discerning and following the Spirit.

Triangle of Ministry

The Triangle of Ministry provides another tool for this journey.

Dick Broholm shared this with us years ago at a seminar I participated in at Andover Newton Seminary. I've found it to be an excellent and easy tool for discernment and discovery.

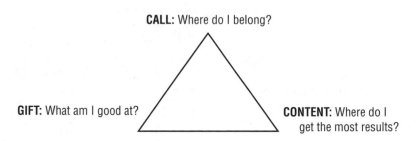

CALL: Where do I belong?

GIFT: What am I good at?

CONTENT: Where do I get the most results?

Leadership can be an exciting or a draining challenge. When leaders are mismatched with other leaders or with congregations, leadership takes on challenges that can be draining and frustrating. On the other hand, when leaders are connected with each other around complementary gifts, callings, and passions, and when the congregation is open to God's leading toward a common mission, then leadership is exciting, invigorating, and fruit-bearing. How does a leader move from just wandering in the malaise of a wilderness assignment to walking amidst a group of soldiers passionate about their mission? Often when leaders lose their way, they become frightened and domineering and start to push rather than lead people forward.

Coaching Questions to Consider

1. What are your discoveries about your call, giftedness, and where you get most results?
2. What can you do to better align your daily activities with your discoveries?
3. Who in your church needs to know about your discoveries?
4. When will you share the information with those significant leaders?
5. What is your next step in this spiritual leadership journey?

Spiritual leadership in a secular age is a challenge at best. Hopefully this chapter has helped you explore some biblical and practical concepts of leadership and coached you through some adjustments in belief or practice that you might need to act upon. Looking into the mirror is a tough but essential assignment. We no longer have the privilege of playing church and impacting this secular world. We must embrace anew the mandate for the church and learn to walk into it and stop wandering in the wilderness. What will make this more of a reality for you and your church?

6

The Methods

Engaging and Impacting without Building Barriers among the Unchurched

Leadership Challenges

"Why are people moving in all around our church but not visiting or joining our church?"

"What goes wrong when I share the plan of salvation with the unchurched, young adult, spiritual travelers in my community?

"What are the barriers I or my church creates that prevent unchurched spiritual travelers from coming to our church?

"How can I create bridges rather than barriers so that spiritual travelers can walk into the church on their spiritual pilgrimage?"

Years ago an unchurched spiritual traveler friend asked me, "Why do churches and church people work so hard building barriers to keep me out rather than bridges to let me in?" What a powerful question that was for me. When I asked him to describe the barriers that were keeping him out of the church, he had his answers all lined up. His question was so powerful that it really birthed this book. My search for answers to his question began as I started looking at myself as a leader, then at my congregation, then at my community of faith, then at my denomination, etc. That journey has produced much of what I will share here.

Jesus' Model with Unbelievers

My church culture and tradition taught me that as a believer I was not to associate with unbelievers. I learned language, behaviors, songs, traditions, and ways of relating to the churched while almost simultaneously I was building barriers between me and the unchurched God was calling me to influence and reach. The language, behaviors, songs, traditions, rituals, etc., that seemed to endear me to the church very often generated gaps between the unchurched and me. For instance, language was and still is a real issue when it comes to relating to the unchurched. They often use language that doesn't fit my church culture and often offends church people. This builds a barrier. On the other hand, the unchurched often misinterpret words like *salvation, grace, sin, repentance.* Or such language communicates our judgment of them, suggesting to them that "we" think we are "better" than "they" are. Thus another barrier emerges. How do Christians remain faithful to their beliefs and traditions without compromising their beliefs and ethics? How can we build bridges of relationships with potential for influencing the spiritual formation of those who are thirsty for health, wholeness, and Christ-centered life? What's a Christian to do?

In John 4, Jesus seems to give us a great model for building bridges instead of barriers with those not part of our church culture. The story of Jesus and the woman at the well provides us a great example of how Jesus approached unbelievers:

- He was on their turf (while she was at the well).
- He approached the unbeliever at a time when she was ready (when she was thirsty and reaching for water).
- He used language they could relate to (the imagery of living water since she was thirsty and drawing water from the well).
- He listened carefully to discern the state of their spiritual journey (knew that she was hurting in her relationships).
- He reflected clearly to the unbeliever what he discerned in order to check his discernment (told her she had had many husbands).

- He offered hope and healing. ("Go and sin no more" provided hope and opportunity for healing if she wanted it and was ready for it.)

Jesus himself knew how it feels to be an outsider looking in. Jesus was often criticized for eating with sinners, slobs, and drunks. His critics looked at everything through their religious eyes and called Jesus a drunkard and glutton. Jesus urges us to excel in loving one another (Jn. 13:1). Jesus declares that we need to love until the end and to trust that He will complete that which He has started in the hearts and lives of those inside and outside the fellowship. Christians must persevere to love persons to the full extent of their need and His grace. This is not a matter of choosing people to love. It is loving those Christ loved, those the church now ignores and judges.

Behaving Properly Toward Outsiders

Churches often need counsel on how to behave toward outsiders and how to build bridges to them. Northerners move in as Southern transplants. Western churches must open their doors to Eastern Yankees. City people invade rural communities, or farmers walk the aisle of urban congregations.

Believers have to earn the right to be heard by the unchurched and to be trusted that they love unconditionally. Only then will the unchurched move beyond religion and cynicism to trust. Many spiritual travelers—unsaved or unchurched persons—do not encounter or receive this type of love. When outsiders see and experience this kind of love, they will want it. Unsaved and unchurched persons can think. They are watching how Christians are responding to the diverse and rapidly changing world.

Paul's writings very often provide guidance for building bridges with those who are different. First Thessalonians 4:9–10 provides the key. These verses challenge us to excel in love even more (God's Word), to see it through. We do not love them just when they earn the love. We love them even when they don't deserve it. We must learn to love one another.

As we move into the twenty-first century, we can't expect to live in this world and not come in contact with unchurched persons. Every turn in life leads us to persons who share little or none of the appreciation for church born into us as the churched culture.

Unfortunately, many Christians develop a very self-absorbed and self-serving lifestyle. We serve each other, take care of each other, and spend time with each other. Many times we do this to the exclusion of the mandate to "Go ye into all the world." We fail to *be* salt, light, and leaven in the world. Such self-centered behavior has earned Christians the reputation as being judgmental, self-serving, pompous, and hypocritical. All too often we tend to get caught up in the extremes and become so preoccupied with persons on the inside of our fellowship that we exclude the very persons from the outside that we are supposed to exist to reach. Biblical truths are challenging a new generation of Christians to be effective in reaching the unchurched generation. These biblical challenges help us repent and realign our behaviors so we might build more bridges than barriers with persons outside our faith tradition.

Move from Building Barriers to Building Bridges

John 17:11–23 captures some valuable truths and practical tips that might help Christians move from building barriers to building bridges. While praying for Himself and then for His disciples, Jesus encounters the challenge to move beyond self-focus to focus on others outside the immediate fellowship. This challenge is a difficult one drawn with a fine line. We do need fellowship with other believers, and we are to carry one another's burdens. But we must not do *just* this. We must not exclude awareness of and engagement with others who are outside the faith or fellowship. When all our talk is God talk, all our friends are God friends, and all our time is spent with other believers, we end up pushing nonbelievers away. We do not push them away consciously. We simply have no time, no space for them in our lives. We lose touch with the real world and isolate and insulate ourselves in our safe sanctuaries and our safe relationships. In essence we often create our own little kingdoms rather than working to build God's realm.

Jesus reminds the disciples and Himself to guard against extremes—not too much in one world or the other. Being a faithful and fruit-bearing believer demands balance in both worlds. John 17:11–18 provides us the final scene of Jesus' prayer life and his last petitions for believers. He prays that "joy might be fulfilled," that we be "kept from the evil one,'" and that believers not be "taken out of the world but to remain in the world but not of the world." He prayed not that we would be isolated from the world, but rather insulated from the evil forces in the world. He further prayed that His disciples be "set apart in the truth," "sent into the world." This makes it very clear to me that Jesus intended for His disciples to build relationships with those in the world—those *unlike* us (unchurched culture people). In fact, it seems clear to me that this is not an option but an essential part of being light, salt, and leaven.

Paul picks up the other extreme side of this debate in 1 Corinthians 5. He challenges Christians not to live so worldly that the world would be shocked and accuse believers of hypocrisy, for then the world would get confused. Christians living among people who are worldly help give those people signs of hope and make them aware they can't change on their own. The worldly quickly see that they have no power within themselves to change their hearts. In fact, it seems fairly clear here that Paul is suggesting that Christians be tough on each other and easy on outsiders. It's a sad reality that the longer we live in the family of God the fewer unsaved or unchurched people we know.

Paul in 1 Corinthians 5:8–10 addresses traditions and rituals of the outsiders and how believers should act around those "pagan" traditions. He seems to suggest that often times we expect the unchurched person to have the same lifestyle as Christians. Christians then expect unchurched persons to live the lives of believers. But it can't happen. We want to change externals before the heart is changed. How unfair to the nonbelievers and unchurched. We cannot expect to change behavior before changing the heart. We cannot expect to change the heart at a distance. We must include them in our fellowship and worship before we can expect them to join our membership. Any other expectations build unfair barriers for unchurched persons. We sing multiple verses of the invitation hymn "Just as I Am," but we really want people to clean up, use our language, and embrace our rituals and traditions before they participate in our worship. We do not afford them time to embrace the gospel and grow in grace. We must lower our expectations and find ways to make the lost or unchurched person feel right at home in our midst.

Bridge-building Tips

Spiritual leadership *through* the body of Christ is seen clearly in 1 Thessalonians 4. In 1 Thessalonians 4:9–12 Paul offers practical tips for behaving properly toward outsiders–those whose thinking, behavior, or traditions are different from yours. We get some very practical bridge-building tips when faced with a diverse and challenging world:

1. **Be quiet** (4:11–12). Lead a quiet life. Too often we feel we must talk and try to verbally convince others we're right. Paul suggests living a quiet life. He even suggests that we mind our own business. He also speaks here about living in community in a responsible fashion. Living life before outsiders so that they might

have respect for you is the challenge believers face in a secular age.

2. **Mind your own business** (4:11–12). Work steadily at your assignment in life. Don't impose your beliefs on others, but be ready to give clear witness of your beliefs by the life you live.

3. **Work with your hands** (4:11). Christians have to earn the right to be heard and to speak into the lives of the unchurched secular culture by working with our hands. The idea in this verse is that people who don't earn their wage forfeit their right to be heard. Walking the walk is just as important as talking the talk of Christianity. Someone gave the illustration that many people are often ready to carry the piano bench when the piano is what needs to be moved. Spiritual leadership in a secular age is about the tough but vital assignment of moving the piano, not just moving the bench.

4. **Conduct yourselves with wisdom following God's teaching** (4:9; compare Col. 4:5). Make the most of the opportunities you are given. Spiritual leadership skills include being intentional about looking for and praying for the teachable moments and divine appointments with persons who are from a different culture or value system. Jesus called us "to observe all things" (Matt. 28:28 KJV).

5. **Act with integrity** (4:11). When our doing comes out of our being rather than our being coming out of our doing, we will be making progress as spiritual leaders in a secular age. Being a person of integrity allows the unchurched and churched persons to watch us and see that our walk and our talk match.

6. **Learn to speak with grace** (4:11–12). Season every word with a little bit of grace, not the whole box. Too often believers pounce on nonbelievers and quote Scriptures—"hit them with the Bible" to make a point. Learning to speak with grace calls for discernment and timing. Rather than trying to make a point or win an argument, we need to try to make a friend and build trust. Christian speech should always reveal Christian love. That applies to the stranger on the street as well as to the personal friend in the pew.

7. **Customize your approach to each person** (4:10). Understand each person has a unique story and comes from a unique place in his or her spiritual journey. Discern where people are in their spiritual journeys, and then validate them in that phase of the journey. Let them see that each phase is just as vital and important a part of the journey as any other phase. Learning to walk with

people on their journey is a critical skill for spiritual leaders in a secular age. You can become Immanuel, "God with Us" for that person.

The Focal Tasks of Postmodern Ministry

Randy, a postmodern spiritual traveler I've been coaching for over a decade, questioned my motives and challenged my attempts to help him many times. I came to understand his behavior when I learned of his journey. He had been abandoned early in life through the untimely death of his mother. Now he was testing me to see if I, too, would abandon him. Many times in exasperation I felt like leaving him alone and finding someone else who would be worth my time and effort. God would not give me the inner permission to abandon Randy, so I persevered. Gradually, I came to see Randy's desire to move forward and how much he needed and wanted help. I had to learn to accept the fact that he needed to test me repeatedly before he was able to accept help. I had to learn to keep walking with him even when we seemed to be going nowhere.

What does the walking with ministry look like? How can you describe the ministry of nonanxious presence for spiritual leaders seeking to minister in a secular age? My experience with Randy helps us answer such questions. When living among and seeking to walk with nonbelievers or persons from a postmodern age, focus on these tasks:

- **Watching and Wondering**—Look for the divine appointments and teachable moments in their lives. These are times when their life circumstances create questions, pinches they need to work through, or beliefs they need to firm up or reexamine. Note that they are watching you, your lifestyle, your habits, and how well you accept them unconditionally. They are learning to trust you before they can learn to trust God. This is a dimension of incarnational theology in which Christians are called to live the Scripture more than to read the Scripture. Nonbelievers often want to see if we will carry the piano bench or move the piano. Sometimes they test us to see if we will really walk with them through their pain, struggle, questions, and confusions.

- **Listening and Learning**—These skills are at the core of the good news and of being an effective spiritual leader in a secular age. The models and words of Paul and Jesus reinforce this for us through their examples and their teachings. Those of us who have been to seminary are most often graded on our ability to talk, not our ability to listen. Talking worked in a church culture. Listening is the skill that works in a secular culture. Being open to learn from them rather than always standing in a teaching posture is critical as well. God can teach us through each other's lives and through the work of God in our lives. Learning to be open to this is critical and challenging.

Listening to and learning of the journey of others has been a challenge for me. Randy was living in much pain and fighting many internal and external battles due to bad decisions he had been and was making. Telling him anything was not working. He needed someone to listen–to give him undivided attention without wanting anything from him in return. He had played relationship games all his life and had to learn to trust me. The pathway to that trust-building was learning to listen. I had to give him time filled with unconditional love. I had to prove I valued who he is and who he can become. I must confess this was a steep learning curve for me at times, but it has paid high dividends as I continue to celebrate the work God is doing in Randy's life.

- **Speaking Your Words with Grace**–Learning to share without judgment is critical in an unchurched secular culture. Speaking words from the heart illustrates grace, when the heart is a place of identification and empathy rather than a place of judgment. We must learn to love the unlovely and to separate the person from behavior we may not like or identify with. This lays a foundation for future conversations and for the development of trust and mutual respect. Persons in the secular world want to see evidence that God works in daily life. Unless they find clear evidence that God moves and acts outside the traditional church times and church places, many from the secular culture pay no attention to God or to God's "people." Thus they see no value in God. When believers find God outside the box of traditional church and learn to live authentically in the world, then the unchurched will begin to restore respect for who we are and who the God is we worship.

- **Just a Little Bit of Salt and a Lot of Grace**–Persons from a church culture tend to be super-evangelistic in attitude and often super-pious. They come across to those who are unchurched as "Bible thumpers" or "religious fanatics." Why? Because they go overboard by being overzealous with religious language or rituals of the faith. Or they express criticism rather than sharing a lot of grace in the midst of persons who often have little or no framework for church culture traditions, language, or rituals. Learning to teach by one's presence rather than one's words becomes a real challenge for many believers. Words are important in communicating our faith and story, and the right to be heard is just as important to those in the postmodern world.

- **Relating to Others with Grace**—Another real challenge in our age is not to judge a book by its cover. We must not stereotype persons who are different from us or different from one another. Many in the postmodern and secular world tend to dress in ways unique to their culture. Often they use their body as art canvas and use jewelry in places many church people find offensive or, at best, confusing. Persons deserve to be treated individually and not lumped into a judgment or assessment about a group—whether involving generation, culture, ethnic background, sexual orientation, or social or economic status.

Creating Thirst in a Postmodern World

As a way of summarizing in practical ways what we've explored from biblical concepts, I want to share ideas for creating thirst in a postmodern world by using the acrostic CARE. Spiritual leadership in a secular culture magnifies the truth that postmoderns don't care how much we know until they experience how much we CARE. Allow me to pose some coaching questions to facilitate acting on these biblical principles.

Coaching Questions to Help You CARE

Context

- Who are the persons God is drawing you to?
- Where are they in their spiritual formation journey?
- What language is best to use to build bridges instead of barriers with these spiritual travelers?
- What are the best questions to ask that build bridges instead of barriers?
- What are the best entry points to create conversation and trust that will build bridges with spiritual travelers?

About Their Journey

- What are their issues/concerns/questions?
- What are the pains/struggles going on in their lives that they want to find meaning in?

- What questions could you ask that would build bridges instead of barriers around their issues?
- How can you best communicate with them biblical truths that inform their journey without building barriers or judging?
- How can you remember it's about their journey and not yours?

Resourceful

- How can you invite the Holy Spirit into this relationship?
- What are the teachable moments you are looking for in this relationship?
- What are the divine appointments God is setting up or you are praying about in this relationship?
- How can you create or be a safe place for the spiritual travelers?
- What print or media resources might be a pathway of nonthreatening education or means of dialogue?

Encourage

- How can you communicate care without judgment?
- What are the ingredients of creating a safe place for spiritual travelers to process their pain, life experiences, and questions?
- What are the ways of affirming their progress without judging their shortcomings?
- How can you communicate believing in them and affirming their progress without building barriers to them finding and taking next steps?
- What are the avenues of encouragement that they are most likely to respond to during difficult days of their journey?

What I'm trying to get at here is that spiritual leadership in a postmodern, post-Christian culture has not only called forth shifts, as in the days of Paul and Jesus. It is challenging the institutional church to rethink mission, methods, mediums, and message. A final illustration of this might be best communicated to church culture leaders when we talk about money and stewardship issues, since that is something valued by the church culture. Here are some suggestions for working *through* the body to accomplish this challenge. As you think through these suggestions, you need to ask yourself two questions. What shifts does this create in my thinking, methods, and mission? How does the new reality differ from what I have traditionally done?

The following list serves as a summary of many of the concepts we've explored in the previous two chapters. The challenge is one familiar to Jesus and to Paul in their journeys as they learned to minister to those who were from cultures different from their own. What behaviors and attitudes create paths that attract, assimilate, disciple, and deploy spiritual travelers?

Creating Paths That Attract, Assimilate, Disciple, and Deploy Adults

- Listen actively and prayerfully for signals about the condition of their hearts and heads.
- Be attentive and prayerful to inconsistencies between what you observe and what you hear from postmodern adults.
- Reflect those experiences and thoughts they are having related to "meaning, purpose of life, and connecting with the universe."
- Learn to build bridges instead of barriers in your relationships with unchurched postmodern persons. Find the places of intersection of beliefs, values, and experiences. Build on those rather than judging deficiencies or trying to "correct them."
- Seek to discern what their passions, values, and callings are that might create entry points for you. These are pathways for investment or partnering in areas that are comfortable for them, benefit them, and provide opportunities for broadening the Christian influence of others who might enter their lives in these venues.
- Ask what they would like to invest in or contribute to. Let them describe how that might look and happen for them.
- Ask if they know of others who might like to partner in such a venture either by financial, prayer, or active support.
- Be consistent in your contact and transparent in your journey through life with them.
- Seek to grow your influence. Find ways to gain trust and respect from them and from others who might be in their sphere of influence. Walk with them as a life coach.
- Invite them, as they are ready and ripe, into deeper levels of conversation, discipling, and investment in fulfilling their calling or passions.
- Invite them to meet other believers who share some of their passions, callings, or concerns to move *their passions* forward.
- Model Christian virtues as you walk into life with them through formal and informal relational experiences.
- Listen for the teachable moments, and watch for the divine appointments that God brings about to move them forward in faith and fulfillment as they align themselves more and more to God's leading and mission.

- Invite them into
  - ~ small groups
  - ~ recreation experiences
  - ~ life passage affirmations and support channels
  - ~ mission experiences
  - ~ music, drama, art experiences
  - ~ holy use of money
  - ~ finding meaning in life
  - ~ faith and work intersections
  - ~ building community and meaningful relationships

A final summary of this chapter causes me to revisit concepts I've previously mentioned from the writings of Tom Bandy. Tom explains the shifts between the modern and postmodern culture and how the church and postmodern spiritual travelers typically respond.

Church	Postmodern Culture
Believe	Belong
Behave	Behave
Belong	Believe

The values of the church culture (generally for those born before 1960) led them to call for persons to **believe** as they did and **behave** the way they did before they were allowed to **belong** in their membership. The postmodern generation (generally born after the 1960s) has such cynicism and distrust that they want to **belong** first and then experience and learn **beliefs** through community. Only then will their **behaviors** change as they grow in belief and community. Quite a shift for the church to deal with, don't you think? The challenge becomes how to keep people over 60 while you reach people under 40. How do you grow leaders and structures that can handle such a strategic and vital assignment? This leads us into the next chapter, "Growing Spiritual Leaders in a Secular Age."

7

The Message

*Growing Spiritual Leaders
in a Secular Age*

Leadership Challenges

"How can we find and develop spiritual leaders in an age of busy adults?"

"What does it take to develop a church's leadership base today?"

"How can we streamline decision making and programming that will accomplish the church's mission and mobilize its membership?"

"Is it possible to be faithful to biblical commands and deal with the declining commitment level of today's adults toward church involvement?"

These questions and others are indicative of issues I hear from church leaders on a frequent basis. This chapter will seek to provide some practical ways of growing spiritual leaders who are faithful *and* fruitful in a secular age.

Developing spiritual leaders *through* the church provides excitement, challenge, and opportunity as we move into a new century. Thus far we have looked at realities the church is facing, and the mission, the medium, and the methods of such an assignment. Now an overview of the message will review the biblical framework and some practical applications for growing spiritual leaders in a secular and postmodern age.

Basic Definitions

Before we begin, let me provide some definitions that will help you move through the material more effectively:

1. **Teleclass**–provides training over the telephone. Telephone bridge lines are available from many sources that allow persons to call into a bridge line number from anywhere in the world to connect with up to thirty persons at a time. The cost is minimal to each caller and allows for networking, dialogue, and coaching around various issues of concern to the callers.

2. **Coach Approach**–is growing in popularity in many industries and ministries due to the growing need for customization and growing leaders. Coaches are trained to listen, ask powerful questions, and move clients and organizations to action to help them achieve their desires and fulfill their agendas. More information available at www.valwoodcoaching.com

3. **Web-based Learning**–uses the Internet as a learning and networking tool. For those who are computer friendly, web cameras provide face-to-face meetings without travel. There are also many interactive CD ROMs and online training programs that provide convenient resources for learning. More information available at www.gotomeeting.com

4. **Online Real Time Threaded Forums**–are another way to network and create learning forums via the Internet. Utilizing a chat room or a formal online real time threaded forum allows persons all across the globe to connect in real time over a given topic.

5. **Face-to-Face Seminars**–are familiar to most. This is where people meet face to face in a room with a facilitator or seminar leader to explore a topic of mutual interest. While this is still popular, it is by no means the only way to meet or create learning experiences in these days of technology.

6. Satellite Links–provide membership with major means of training. Such a membership allows satellite hook-ups that facilitate a feed right to your television set. One of the most popular links for churches is www.ccnonline.net

Four Disciple-making Phases in the Life of Jesus

The biblical framework overviewed here comes from the life and disciple-making model of Jesus. His spiritual leadership is captured in four biblical concepts and phrases that worked in his secular and pluralistic culture and are certain to work in ours. Each of these concepts can be found in each of the gospels. This widespread occurrence gives clear evidence of their value in the ministry of Jesus. Jesus found himself in the midst of a pluralistic, pagan, secular age in which many were loyal to religious traditions and rituals, but the masses were practicing pagans, following sexual gods. Sounds like our day. So let's look at His model of growing spiritual leaders through a summary of each phase of disciple making.

Come and See (John 1:38–39)

Jesus knew that in a pre–Christian and secular world He would have to attract and build relationships before anything else could happen. Consequently, the first phase of his ministry was usually meeting persons on their turf in places where they were likely more comfortable with their environment than He was. He went to weddings, parties, fishing trips, business gatherings, and community-wide festivals. There he sought to find language that would communicate to those he was with rather than use religious language. While clear about His boundaries, He was all about building bridges rather than barriers. He encountered Nicodemus, the secret believer, under the cover of night. He welcomed conversations with the "unclean" woman with the issue of blood, the "foreign" woman at the well, the blind beggar, the tax collector considered a traitor to his country. He also called the salt-of-the-earth fisherman, strong-headed Peter. Finally, from heaven he contacted Christian-killing Saul and turned him into church-planting Paul. The list goes on.

At this point in their journey Jesus wasn't calling them to embrace his religious language, traditions, dress, or rituals. He wanted to attract their interest and build a relationship with them. He sought to include them in places where they could belong.

Come and Follow Me (Mark 1:16–17)

Having attracted their interest and curiosity, Jesus had fellowship with them. At that point he was ready to engage them at their point of interest. Once a relationship was in place, Jesus walked with persons to the next level of their spiritual journey as he asked them to "come follow me." This phase is all about answering questions and responding to issues they raised. He prayed for and worked toward divine appointments and teachable moments. When they asked, "Lord teach us to pray," he captured that moment in their lives as a way of leading them forward in faith.

Responding to their questions and issues was a way to lead them to develop spiritual life disciplines. Coaching questions were key during this phase of growing spiritual leaders. "Who do people say that I am?" he asked. Such a question invited Peter and others to make an internal decision and commitment.

During this time of following, Jesus also modeled for them what spiritual leadership looked like. His behaviors, actions, attitudes, and relationships were something His followers observed as they followed Him in all arenas of life on a daily basis. Such mentoring and discipling were critical in their journey and in His strategy. Jesus did not expect perfection of those who followed Him. He looked for sincerity and faithfulness. When followers proved themselves capable and faithful, he invited them to leadership. They had been observing him; now he would be observing them in leadership roles as he coached them forward in faith and function.

Come and Be with Me (Mark 3:13–14)

Come be with me essentially becomes "come be me." The follower becomes a leader of others and one who emulates the virtues, teachings, behaviors, and lifestyle of Christ. They can be like Christ in these ways because they have observed and learned about these ways in previous ventures with Christ. Such an incarnational phase of life is the essence of the good news. God came to earth in human form so that others might see, walk with, and experience Him in the daily events of life.

This phase of leadership training is about deepening, integrating, and personalizing those beliefs and skills to which they are committing themselves. Jesus continues to be around for coaching and for question and answer sessions, but basically they are in an apprentice relationship.

Learning to represent His presence in various phases and stages of life demands time and patience on the part of all concerned. Walking with Jesus and learning what it is for Him to be Lord of all of your life is a life stage and life change that calls forth what we were created to be. This phase is about owning who He created us to be and living into our destiny and our full potential. Here is the place and experience where we find and experience all the abundance life has to offer. This is not to say it's perfection and without struggle. In fact, it is only in the pain and struggle that many lessons are learned and that the faithfulness of Christ in those experiences is made clear.

Come Abide in Me (John 15:4)

Jesus declares the "field test" and apprenticeship over. He must physically leave, but he promises to leave His Spirit. Thus we will then be able to do *greater things* than he has done because we have been with Him. The abiding relationship hinges on prayer and on learning to live into and from the spiritual life disciplines that have been taught and caught as they walked with Christ. Abiding has an intentionality to it: being intentional about the disciplines, the fellowship with other believers, reading and living lessons from scripture, and being salt, light, and leaven in the church and as the church in the world. What a privilege! What a gift! What a responsibility! What a challenge!

This quick review of this biblical framework is captured on the following chart about the "Distinctives in Each Disciple-making Phase," which comes from the work of Bill Hull and Bob Gilliam of T-Net International. A more thorough treatment of these phases can be found in their writings.[1]

One Size Does Not Fit All

The various phases of disciple-making provide a framework for ministering amidst diversity and challenge. Living and leading in a pluralistic, fast-paced, secular world reinforces for us that one size does not fit all. It never has, but it certainly does not now. Jesus' disciple-making strategy recognized this challenge. Our strategies must acknowledge this key element in disciple-making, too. Persons coming from a pagan world come to this spiritual journey from many different experiences, places, traditions, family systems, belief systems, and skill sets. Growing leaders means taking them from where they are and moving them forward to their full potential. Such takes time, patience, energy, commitment, perseverance, faith, conviction, dedication, and much prayer. This process is not nearly as linear or clear-cut as many would like. This process of making leaders is more grey and calls forth more discernment of the Spirit's movement in the world, in your life, and in the lives of those being discipled.

Growing people and leaders in a secular age is much tougher than the same task conducted during the church culture age, when most had positive impressions of church, God, Bible, pulpit, preachers,

Distinctives in Each Disciple-making Phase

	Come See	Follow Me	Be with Me	Remain in Me
Scripture	John 1:38–39	Mark 1:16–17	Mark 3:13–14	John 15:4
Intent	• To attract and win to himself • To build beliefs and some priorities	• To train for task • To build habits and basic character	• To deploy as disciple-makers • To deepen basic habits and develop new ones	• To replace Himself • To continue the development of Christ-likeness without forgetting the basics
Disciples' Involvement	• Mostly watching • Somewhat involved • Did not lead	• Somewhat watching • Quite involved • Did not lead	• Quite involved • Did a lot of leading	• Involved in leading leaders
Commitment	• Casual occasional attendance	• Constantly present	• Willing to die/give all to follow as long as Jesus was present	• Intrinsically motivated to the death
Content		• Mostly the same	• Truth but deepening	• With time
Summary	• Tell them what • Tell them why	• Show them how • Do it with them	• Let them do it • Deploy them	• Multiplication • Continual growth

From T-NET International Leadership Training—Used by Permission from Bob Gilliam, President. For more information call 1–800–995–5362 or visit www.tnetwork.com and read *Jesus Christ the Disciplemaker, The Disciple Making Church* by Bill Hull, Revell Press. www.tnetwork.com

etc. Now those positive impressions are absent for many in our land. Learning to listen, to respect others, not to judge, and to persevere in the face of opposition or steep learning curves pays high dividends and calls forth a deeper faith and more steady walk with God. Discernment is a constant challenge for the disciple-maker. Learning to discern where to draw the lines, to maintain the integrity of the good news, and not to build barriers is challenging at best. Also, learning to build relationships and trust so as to build bridges for the next phase of the journey calls forth deeper discernment and faith. If we don't attract people, we can never reach them with the good news. If they don't trust us, they will never trust our faith or our God.

How does this reality flesh itself out in structure and in practice instead of theory? Well, I'm glad you asked. The remainder of this chapter will seek to overview applications of this in the real world of church and ministry in a missionary environment.

Come and See Practices

Several years ago while struggling with the practical expressions of Jesus' disciple-making model in the twenty-first century, I was in a movie theater viewing *The Green Mile.* At the end of what proved to be a movie full of spiritual themes, I noticed that few people in the theater had left during the credits. They sat as if in a "holy hush," processing what they had just seen. After all, who wants to watch the credits of a movie. So I sat and listened, observed, and prayed. As the group started leaving, I overheard many conversations threaded with spiritual questions and epiphanies. Wow!!! What was going on here? This could be a "come and see" experience, but how do you capture it and build relationships around their questions and issues? Such became an obsession for me. Then I decided to build a relationship with the movie theater manager and staff so I could present an idea. Long story short, through the help of the management I purchased an ad at the beginning of movies with a spiritual theme (and there are many these days). I tried to create a safe place for spiritual dialogue for unchurched persons. I soon discovered others who were just as passionate about connecting movies and spiritual formation. See my Web site for excellent resources. My favorite Web site for this ministry, which networks churches and believers involved in this ministry, is www.hollywoodjesus.com. Below you will find an outline of my "come and see" ministry and some of the coaching questions I use to facilitate such a dialogue and relationship-building venture.

Spiritual Formation and Secular Movies

Creating a Safe Place for Spiritual Dialogue

1. Invitation to the Dialogue
   a. Advertisement that runs at the beginning of the movie: "If Church Doesn't Work For You and You Desire to Dialogue about the Spiritual Themes in This Movie, Meet in Coffee Shop at xxxxxx."
   b. Build partnership with theater and coffee shop management; try to make this a win-win for everyone.
   c. Reduce as much anxiety as possible.
2. Creating a Safe Place for Spiritual Dialogue
   a. Assess the group's spiritual appetite. Based on the number in the group, you might invite them to break into small groups for this dialogue. Sometimes this doesn't seem to be appropriate or safe for some. Follow your intuition and discernment at this point.
      i. "What brings you to this dialogue?"
      ii. "What would make this a meaningful experience for you?"
      iii. "What would reduce the meaningfulness of this experience for you?"
   b. If introductions seem appropriate, introduce by first names; do not mention church affiliation unless you have basically a churched crowd.
   c. Don't set anyone up as "spiritual authority." Provide open questions to discern what phase of discipleship they are in and where they may be interested in moving. (Come and See, Come and Follow Me, Come and Be with Me, Come Abide in Me)
3. Provide each participant with two blank 3 by 5" cards to use as they choose. They may want to write questions for the group, note down dialogue they want to recall, write their contact info, e-mail, etc., for you. Two cards are provided in case they want to keep one and give you one. Provide them some contact info to maintain contact with you; e-mail is usually best.
4. Review and suggest Web sites that might help connect faith and media for them. (See my Web site for current listing of resources.)
5. Here are some coaching questions that facilitate a nonthreatening but meaningful spiritual formation dialogue for the spiritual travelers:
   a. What was most meaningful for you in the film?

b. Can you help us understand how this was meaningful for you?

c. What questions did the film leave you pondering?

d. How do you plan to find answers to these questions?

e. Could this group or someone in this group possibly help with this search for deeper meaning?

f. What feelings did the movie create for you?

g. What memories were called to mind from viewing the movie?

h. What questions did the movie create for you? your belief system?

i. What was missing for you in the movie?

j. What gaps did the movie create for your belief system?

k. What life experiences have you had that mirror in some way the movie themes?

l. If you could rewrite the ending, how would you rewrite it?

m. What character in the movie did you relate to the most? (the least?)

n. What are you taking away from the movie viewing or this group dialogue?

o. What might be some next steps for you as you move forward in your spiritual journey?

p. What narrative from your belief system informs or is challenged by the movie?

q. How are you encountering truth in the movie, and how does it intersect with your belief system?

r. What are the stories and principles for living from your belief system that are magnified or challenged in the movie?

s. How do you plan to deal with these realities or challenges?

What a great time I've had with this ministry, and how God has blessed it. We follow this up with online dialogue and lunch gatherings. We are moving to some home small group experiences. God is up to something. Many churches approached this movie ministry during the massive release of *The Passion of the Christ.* Churches rented movie theaters. Other churches rented space in the mall outside of a movie theater to create "a gathering place" for movie-goers to dialogue about their movie experience. This experience proved so life-changing for one group, that even after *The Passion of the Christ* was over, they continued the ministry in Columbia Mall in Columbia, S.C.

Coaching Questions to Consider

1. What are you learning about "come and see" structures and experiences?

2. What passions and opportunities are available to you through your passions or your community gatherings? Remember these are "as you go," not another layer of activity for you.
3. Who might share a similar interest and could help birth this ministry?
4. What barriers might get in your way?
5. Who can help you resolve these challenges, or what plans can you make to remove or minimize the barrier?
6. What are you willing to do and by when?

Come and Follow Me Expressions

The "come and follow me" phase is built on the questions and agendas of those being discipled. Looking for the divine appointment or teachable moment for the leader in training is part of the customizing challenge. Jesus made himself available in formal and informal settings with those he was discipling so as to practice "as you go" discipleship. He went fishing, shared meals, went to parties and weddings, and engaged in business conversations with his followers.

Developing leaders is a challenging assignment for those in denominational and judicatory service, as well as for those in local church ministries. We all face many of the same challenges brought on by diversity, pluralism of beliefs, and backgrounds. Once relationships have been attracted and formalized to some degree, it's time for the next steps of leadership formation.

To illustrate how the "come and follow me" phase might be expressed in an organization, consider a story from my professional world. For the last several years the staff on which I serve has been in a constant state of reorganization and redesign to help make us more effective in ministering to a twenty-first–century world. We are trying to get a handle on how to develop leaders who are busy. We are exploring convenience of training through a variety of delivery systems. Some of our "customers" are computer friendly and desire on-demand and real time training in the convenience of their home or office. Others want face-to-face gatherings in their local culture. They seek something customized just for them. There's so few of us on staff and such a diversity of opportunity. What are we to do?

We are gradually developing a plan suited to our constituency. Carrying out the "come and follow me" phase in a local church would mean creating programs, ministries, and relationships where spiritual life skills and disciplines could be learned, experienced, and evaluated.

It might be a small group ministry of men, women, or couples who are seeking to learn how to pray, or something about how the Bible was written and how to study the Bible. Another expression would be a mission experience where persons join together to meet the needs of those in their community or across the world by sharing from their spiritual journey or their resources to help others.

Designing a learning and growth experience that is customized to the learner is a vital feature of this phase of developing leaders. Every church and individual will have unique needs, learning styles, time availability, and personality style. What are the ingredients of an effective plan to help learners and followers grow forward as they learn by following the lives and teachings of others?

An illustration of this from an organization's perspective might be helpful. The staff on which I serve is building a training plan around multiple tasks, multiple tiers of needs, and multiple skill sets for the leaders in training we serve.

Based on feedback over the last several years, the following plan has emerged as another step toward a customized, convenient, and cost-effective means of training leaders of leaders. I suspect many of your churches are engaged in similar assessments and reorganization efforts. Maybe the grid that is guiding some of our efforts might offer you suggestions and framework for rethinking your ministry. I am certainly not suggesting our framework is the only framework, but we are finding help by exploring the following chart. This also helps move us toward more of a learning organization and coaching culture that maximizes the expertise of practitioners and field consultants and values the diversity of churches, leader skill sets, and indigenous needs. As a church leader, consider what type of organization God is calling you to create and what needs your "customers" are voicing. See if these concepts and delivery systems offer insight for you.

Coaching Questions to Consider

1. What are you learning about "come and follow me" structures and experiences?
2. What barriers are preventing you from aligning your structures and leadership experiences around this phase?
3. Who can help you remove the barriers and design new experiences?
4. What are you willing to do and by when?

I recently encountered a church that was seeking to build "come and see" structures to teach engaged and newlywed couples the basics

Training Model for Leader of Leaders Training	
Criteria for Training Leaders Request	**Various Delivery Systems for Leaders of Leaders**
Convenience of time, place, and accessibility to leaders	**Teleclass** designed to share information around focused needs
User-friendly for leaders	**Coach Approach**—leader agenda drives the individual or group coaching conversation designed to move people from where they are to where they desire to be
Learning style sensitivity—visual, auditory, experiential	**Web-based Learning/Coaching** that includes instructional learning and telephone or Webcast
Saves money and time related to travel, overnight fees, conference fees	**Online Real Time Threaded Forums** hosted by trained consultant who can add value to the leader's need and connect him or her to an affinity network
Provides personal attention from practitioners and primary leadership	**Face-to-Face Regional Seminars** designed by network and led by appropriate consultant or coach
Network builder among persons or organizations related to leaders' needs	**Satellite links,** Webcasts, partnership ventures, and resourcing between associations and parachurch organizations

of building a healthy, faithful marriage. This was a required course for all those being married in the church or by the pastor and staff. It was considered part of the pre- and post-marital counseling. The "come and follow me" was built around mentoring relationships with others who had proven to have healthy marriages and were willing to be a mentoring couple with these newlyweds for one year. They played together, prayed together, studied together, worshiped together, and shared heart stories and life experiences. What a great illustration of how a church can create experiences, classes, and relationships to facilitate the "come and see" phases of disciple-making.

Come Be with Me (or Be Me) Experiences and Structures

"Come be with me" holds within it the principle and fruits of multiplication and the true essence of discipleship. Once the person has been attracted and apprenticed, then that disciple is ready for leadership. This involves fleshing out what they have learned from previous training opportunities and experiences. This phase of disciple-making can be experienced in a variety of ways in and through the life of the community of faith. Let me share some ideas that could be lived out through a music ministry in a local church. Review each of the ideas. Decide which phase of disciple-making each suggestion provides a framework and experience for—"come and see"; "come and follow me"; "come and be with me." This is a good review exercise but will hopefully also illustrate how each phase can be implemented in the life of a traditional ministry. The essence of growing spiritual leaders in a secular age has much to do with intentionality. How might the intentionality of design, leadership, and curricula assist a local congregation's music ministry develop leaders and grow disciples? Here are some thoughts to consider.

Building a Disciple-making Worship and Arts Ministry

Options to consider. Place a check beside those you are currently doing well. Circle those ideas you feel might have possibilities in your setting, and prioritize how and when you might introduce them. Indicate beside each idea what disciple-making phase seems to be indicated by each idea.

Suggestion for Programming	Disciple-making Phase
Design each choir, ensemble, drama group as a disciple-making group.	
Lead ministry participants to assess their spiritual formation and set spiritual formation goals.	
Create and model accountability atmosphere in all ministry groups and relationships.	
Use worship, ensembles, choirs, drama teams, etc., as possible entry points for the nonbeliever and unchurched persons.	
Lead, as a role model, spiritual formation experiences (Bible study, text story analysis, theological reflection, etc.) in rehearsals and fellowship.	
Provide a library of resources for ministry participants that would equip them, stretch them, minister to them.	

Suggestion for Programming	Disciple-making Phase
Challenge participants consistently in spiritual life disciplines. Allow them to share their stories and experiences with other participants and the congregation. Personal experiences create a great worship atmosphere.	
Create ministry teams through your ministry that can penetrate the community during special events— holidays, community events, street festivals, funerals, weddings, anniversaries, dedications for babies, houses, businesses, etc.	
Balance each ministry group with mentors, coaches, or team leaders. Think of passions, callings, giftings, and spiritual condition.	
Create a permission-giving atmosphere in which participants are encouraged to dream, pray, and follow God's leading without having to jump through many hoops.	
Build healthy partnerships and alliances with community organizations, schools, businesses, county agents, and other churches of all denominations that have as an intentional element disciple-making, outreach, and/or community transformation.	
Explore community or business events that you might pray about. If God leads, offer resources that would build relationships and strengthen their event. (This might be free service or an avenue of fund raising.)	
Create intergenerational experiences in which the old teach the young and vice versa. This might include various arts, crafts, sharing of music styles, etc.	
Create regular hands-on mission experiences for each aspect of worship and arts ministry. This provides an opportunity for team building and ministering beyond the walls of the church.	
Survey the community, and intentionally work to design regular disciple-making, nonthreatening entry points (places or experiences that are easy for them to embrace or be a part of) for the nonchurched, but spiritually thirsty persons.	
Find the most nonthreatening atmosphere in town, and develop a way to build a disciple-making ministry there through your gifts.	

Suggestion for Programming	Disciple-making Phase
Share consistently in your church business meetings, church fellowship and family meetings, and worship how God is using your ministry to disciple believers and nonbelievers in your community.	
Create a music camp or teaching situation targeting the nonbelievers and nonchurched persons.	
Create spiritual formation teams within your ministry whose members will be point persons for the disciple-making dimension of this ministry. Each person would be a champion for disciple-making in the group.	

My next steps in building a healthy disciple-making ministry through worship and arts will be…

1. _____

2. _____

3. _____

Abide in Me Experiences and Structures

The "abide in me" phase of developing leaders is about sustaining and multiplying that which one learns and experiences in previous phases of training. Granted, these phases are developmental and appear somewhat linear, but you must realize that the process is not as linear as it might appear. As people experience new encounters, they may weave in and out of these phases as new life experiences challenge faith, learnings, and growth.

Sustaining and developing one's learning beyond a classroom or learning experience is a challenge in this fast-paced world. What are some ways of sustaining the learning experience and integrating it into life?

- Enlist accountability from trusted persons for life change. An accountability person walks with you through life challenges and changes and is someone you trust to mirror reality and offer encouragement, correction, and counsel.
- Enlist a personal coach to help you integrate what you are learning into life, to walk with you and ask well-timed questions to help

you move toward life goals and through learning curves. Visit www.valwoodcoaching.com or www.onpurposeministry.com for tips on finding such coaches.

- Maintain a daily or weekly journal of what you've learned.
- Set action-oriented goals after each learning experience, and enlist accountability for acting upon the goals. Coaches and accountability persons are enlisted to help grow you forward.
- Build online or teleconference accountability groups or learning communities to sustain and integrate new learnings into a variety of life experiences.

Coaching Questions to Consider

1. What are you learning about growing spiritual leaders in a secular age?
2. How would you as a church leader evaluate your current structures, ministries, and programs in light of these four phases of disciple-making and leadership development?
2. Which insight could you act on that would bring the greatest positive shift in your leadership and programming?
3. What barriers exist to making such shifts?
4. Who could help you in making these shifts in focus, programming, or framework for ministry?
5. What are you willing to do and by when?

The next chapter will explore how to disciple busy adults who are from various generations, have a broad base of learning styles, and are only going to give their spiritual formation and church activities a limited amount of time.

8

The Mandate

Discipling Busy Adults and Newcomers

Leadership Challenges

"How can we disciple adults who are in dual-career marriages, trying to expose their children to every social activity in town, and who only give the church so much of their time?" questioned a frustrated pastor.

"What options do we have for discipling adults? They are not coming to our Sunday night classes anymore!" exclaimed a concerned discipleship leader.

The Challenge of Discipling Today's Adults

"Go and make disciples" is a simple biblical phrase that is an increasingly challenging mandate to fulfill. Finding the right time, place, resource, leader, and curriculum continues to be a pressing challenge for discipling today's busy adults. Families and adults are changing drastically and so is the world we live and work in. Sixty percent of today's adults are considered single by the current census—this reality alone leaves many singles with busy lives, having to work feverishly as they are engaging in multitasking. Dual-career marriages are prevalent. The home schooling movement is consuming the time and energy of other adults. Still other adults are caring for the increasing population of aging parents. Other adults are climbing the career ladder and work fifty to sixty hours a week or more. Other adults are involved in multiple leadership roles in the community and in church that call them to expend time and energy in meetings and in performing multiple tasks. In other words many adults, if not most, find they have a decreasing amount of discretionary time. Also, the learning styles of adults seem to be shifting, though we still learn best when we *need* to learn something rather than when someone *tells* us to learn something. Many churches are still expecting adults to come to the church for Sunday night discipleship training sessions. While that still works in some churches, for most adults it doesn't work and is not likely to work for them for some time in the future. What are the structures and relationships that are being created that disciple today's busy adults? Let's explore some in this chapter. What will work for you? your church? your judicatory? your association? your peers?

Building Relationships Is Essential

We are now living in a different culture than twenty or thirty years ago. Some have suggested we are in a high tech world calling for high touch relationships. Others are talking about building global relationships through cyberspace. Still others are suggesting that the traditional family that is connected biologically is giving way to the creation of surrogate families and "urban tribes." In earlier days discipleship and church life were built around programs, buildings, staff, and centralized worship. Cultural shifts have now created an atmosphere in which relationships are essential. Now we have to earn the right to share our spiritual journey.

Somewhere in the cultural shifts, many adults have lost trust in other people. Front porches were replaced by air-conditioned houses, which keeps us inside in front of computers or televisions that take our attention away from each other. Now we have to learn to rebuild community, learn again how to build trustworthy friendships and family type relationships that are more healthy than dysfunctional. The church has a great opportunity to help adults learn to rebuild and recreate their world and their lives. How then can we create and maximize teachable moments and life-transforming experiences for today's and tomorrow's adults?

Framework for Discipleship in the Twenty-first Century

If you are interested in seeing a strategic model for local church, judicatory, or diocese, visit www.discipleshipteam.org, designed as a framework that represents the best of what I am observing about how discipleship is being done these days. You will note the presentation categorizes around four *P*s—*P*ulpit-oriented approach; *P*rogram-oriented approach; *P*erson-oriented approach; *P*rocess-oriented approach. The following suggestions for discipling busy adults can fit under various parts of these approaches, and some can be adapted to fit into more than one approach. What will work best for you? If this is not a need, then maybe you need to explore the possibilities of decentralizing discipleship and moving it beyond the walls and traditional programs.

Decentralize Discipleship Opportunities

"As you go...make disciples..." is part of the Great Commission. This is taking on a fresh meaning into today's rapid-paced world. In the church culture of the last decades church and discipleship were primarily done in a centralized way in a centralized location. Today, in our secular culture, we return to the days of Acts and the founding of the New Testament church. We are called to "learn to be salt, light and leaven in the world." We are called to learn to do and to be disciples *as* we go into various arenas of life. We are learning to go into parenthood, into the workplace, into our leisure activities, into the lives of our children's activities, into our school systems, into our government and community activities.

Discipling busy adults calls for churches, associations, and judicatories to determine the best ways to decentralize discipleship opportunities. Jesus himself modeled this beautifully with his disciples—he met them in the fishing boat, in the marketplace, on the seashore, at weddings and parties in the community. So what might this look like in our world? What discipling relationships and structures might be created to disciple our busy adults in an effective life-transforming way? Consider the following ideas:

1. **Networking with Fellow Christians through Computer Modems**—Much discipleship is happening around the world as persons with home and business computers begin to network with other Christians and non-Christians. Computer communication revolves around dialogues about business ethics, church/state relationships, seeking divine direction for modern issues/problems in the family, church, business, and community.

2. **Use of Videos, Computer CDs, and DVDs**–Use media to go to where the disciples are, in their homes, offices, vacation homes, cars, boats, etc. Resources are available that speak to issues today's adults/youth/children are seeking guidance on. Our society is infiltrated with media that bombards each of us daily, through television, radio, movies, etc. We must use the media effectively to disciple adults/youth/children.

3. **Use of Audiocassettes, Audio CDs or Downloads**–Again, take the message to the people. With portable audioplayers of various types commonplace almost everyone has an ongoing contact with ways/places to listen to teachings. Many pastors' sermons, conference leaders' lectures, and books are available in a variety of formats for use at the "teachable moments" in people's lives with very effective results.

4. **Use of Support Groups**–Groups concerned with specific needs are another viable way to disciple adults/youth/children. The teachable moments for adults are when they *need* to *learn.* When they are asking questions of faith is the time for us to support them in their faith through grouping people of similar need together to seek God's direction and mutual support from the body of Christ.

5. **Travel/Leisure Time**– Church leaders can challenge people to use the media resources available as they commute to and from work, or even as they travel to their vacation sites. Plant the seed and create the "accountability relationships" that will help them focus some of their driving or flying time for spiritual development. Persons who travel frequently can take advantage of technology to "find time" for spiritual formation while traveling or commuting. Then, because many of us have access to the Internet, phones, etc., we can dialogue with others around similar teaching tools that we share "as we go."

6. **Dialogical Sermons**– provide pathways for discipling. Such sermons must be delivered from God's word to a perceived human/world need. They must deal with current issues from a Christian perspective. After the sermon *provide a time to dialogue* with the listeners so as to facilitate a group/one-on-one discipleship process.

7. **Narrative Theology** *(using the biblical story and our personal stories as avenues of dialogue around life-transforming truths)*– The use of such narrative opens doors for relevant Bible study that can facilitate discipleship. People we are discipling can begin

Bible study by finding themselves in the story and then seeking direction from God through *God's* story. Narrative study facilitates personal growth in the family—*the cradle of our theology*—and in the community of faith: the people of God, wherever we find one another.

8. **Spiritual Direction**—It may seem that spiritual direction is a lost art/discipline among modern believers. Spiritual direction offers searching persons a safe place in a relationship to explore struggles and to discern and claim how God may be moving in their lives. It can provide a ministry to those many adults who are "cocooning in their homes," struggling alone with the issues of faith and real life. Spiritual direction can be done by any child of God who is trained in the discipline. It can be done one-on-one, with families, in vocational groupings, or in groups of fellow Christians.

9. **Retreats/Seminars/Workshops**— Such events offer excellent short-term or long-term discipline for adults. In today's world of "pleasure seekers," leisure fanatics, and people reluctant to commit to long-term obligations, retreats offer much incentive. Find a nice, close—yet away from everyday schedules and concerns—retreat house/center and deal relationally and didactically with current issues. Work to integrate our faith with those issues. Such a retreat or workshop offers great potential for discipling adults.

10. **Telephone Discipling**—This powerful tool for discipling is convenient and serves to "touch base," to offer support, to create or deal with teachable moments of life. It provides an easy way to follow up on tapes, articles, etc., that have been shared through mail or computer.

11. **Discipling at Meal Times**—Meals are much-overlooked opportunities for effective discipleship for busy adults. Invite families, work associates, family members, church members, etc., to share in groups or one-on-one a meal in a restaurant, a home, etc., to focus on cultivating spiritual life development. This discipleship strategy requires accountability as well as budget support.

12. **Intergenerational Experiences**— Bringing together people of different ages can be a very effective discipline tool in today's world. So many need time with people of different ages, as we learn from the aged and the young about the issues of life and faith. Many of the ideas above can be effectively used as intergenerational experiences.

13. **Christian Coaching**–Christian coaching is not about resolving issues for the past, as is counseling, but rather about helping move people to the future and to action that is in line with their belief systems.[1]

Integrate Spiritual Formation with Life Experiences

Discipling does not come in one-size-fits-all packages. Discipling must be tailored to each individual. You cannot simply write out a diet of prayer, Bible study, meditation, worship, and ministry and expect a postmodern to follow it and grow in spiritual formation. Spiritual formation for the modern disciple comes through connecting life experiences with spiritual resources. You may employ a variety of strategies as you help disciple a person in the pre-conversion or early post-conversion stage of their spiritual formation.

Life coaches provide "as you go" formats for discipling adults in the midst of life's teachable moments. Coaches have their own specialties. You can find parenting coaches, care-giver coaches, food coaches, leadership coaches, teaching coaches, calling coaches, and the list goes on. Coaching is about moving people through the gaps of their knowledge or experience. Coaching provides space and time for adults to draw from the presence of the Holy Spirit in their lives. Coaching helps adults move from frustration to action and intentional living–a disciplined life.

I've been engaged in coaching in an intentional way for the last five years and am finding it to be the most exciting and fruit-bearing modality of ministry that I've experienced in my twenty-plus years of professional ministry.

Teachable moments provide entry points and create opportunity for discipleship. Learning to listen for and discern these moments is a needed skill for today's leaders. The church needs a group of mentors, coaches, and small group opportunities available to direct persons through these teachable moments.

The "Faith at Work" movement is gaining momentum daily. Most adults spend the majority of their waking hours at work each week. Adults are looking for ways to connect their faith and their work. Seeking ways to connect Monday and Sunday worlds is critical. Building networks, curricula, small groups, online groups, and learning community and forums for this purpose is a way of building bridges between what I call the "*gathered* and the *scattered* church" as we seek to learn to *be* salt, light, and leaven in the world.[2]

Transformational Work Teams are collaborative efforts between believers, community members, church members, businesses, profit, and nonprofit organizations to help bring about personal and community transformation. Engaging in and learning to build such communities offer excellent opportunities for discipling "as we go." Such involvement creates opportunities for influencing the system and seasoning the decisions and projects with the values and presence of believers and the Christian witness. It also often provides bridge-building opportunities for building trust, mutual respect, and understanding of the diversity of people groups and belief systems we now live in the midst of and are challenged to love.[3]

Online or face-to-face learning communities offer excellent ways to stay connected, take advantage of teachable moments, and enjoy real-time learning and community. Churches are just now beginning to see this, but the next generation and their children are tied to and connected by the Web already. How can we use the Internet for online learning or as a follow-up to face-to-face learning community experiences?

Spiritual transformation beyond church events is a real challenge for most churches today. This is certainly a place where those who share the passion for discipling busy adults can plug in. Once an event is over–whether a "*gathered* or *scattered* church event"–we need a plan to sustain the learning gleaned from the experience. What venue might be created to help network, sustain, and move forward the convictions, communities, or new learnings a person has experienced during the event? What teams might be needed to birth and manage such discipleship venues? What will be the criteria of success for each of these discipling venues?

The realities are challenging institutionally based models of disciple-making on all fronts. George Barna's research confirms for us that there is an ever-increasing number of adults not participating in church while at the same time there's an ever-increasing spiritual thirst in our nation. Barna declares that the number of unchurched adults has increased 92 percent since 1991.[4] How do we reconcile such a statistic with the mandate of the great commission? Maybe we need to try other avenues of disciple-making and growing spiritual leaders. We could begin by modeling a different model of disciple-making for those interested, exploring, or choosing to join our community of faith.

What are the next steps for discipling busy adults in your influence?[5]

New Member Assimilation for Busy Adults

Most adults in our culture are not involved in an institutionally based church.[6] Many of those who are attracted to traditional church and choose to join lose interest and drop out within the first 6 to 8 weeks. This usually happens because they are not properly assimilated into the life and ministry of the congregation. If a traditional church offers any kind of extended new member training plan, the plan usually focuses on making good churchmen and churchwomen of the new members. This training usually makes certain the newcomers know the church denominational affiliation, church programming, church stewardship needs, and doctrinal preferences. Those who really do a thorough job help the newcomers find their spiritual gifts and engage them in mission and ministry. While all of this has its place, many of today's adults are just "too busy" to participate in this extended orientation and training up front. Most adults are looking for relationships and community to link them to the church rather than doctrinal purity and institutional concerns. So how can we best assimilate these busy adults?

Assimilation Begins before They Join

In the '60s and '70s people came to church for relationships. Today, people must have relationships before they come to church. That is, people most often do not come to church unless they already have a friendship relationship with someone in the church. Adults are highly mobile today. Family systems are more fractured and blended. Work styles have shifted in many homes. Consequently, many people live lonely lives. What adults want, but don't know how to get, are friends of the heart. What many adults encounter are dysfunctional persons, fear-based or shamed-based persons trying to discover meaning in life after a time of brokenness. How can the church reach out to such people? Several possibilities offer themselves:

- **Small groups** can be and are often a great place to begin assimilation before a person actually joins the church. The small group often meets in a neutral place, usually a home, which is less threatening to the unchurched than the church building itself.
- **Casual conversations** and relationships are another place assimilation begins. Church members become friends in the workplace, around leisure activities, or through community experiences.
- **Internet is a place of connecting** for many. It's a place where people can choose to be real to test the waters of a potential friendship. Unfortunately, many church people have given over this form of connection to those who use the Web for evil rather than good. Build online forums for a group who shares a similar interest.

- **Cellular phones are great ways to stay connected** and build relationships. Now there are phone plans for friends that allow you to stay connected in significant ways–even as you travel with your job or for leisure. Phone bridge lines are great ways of building community, sharing learnings, and developing networks. They are time savers and conveniences for busy adults.
- **Clubs** offer places for relationship-building and for assimilation to begin before people actually join the church. Why not offer a recreational trip, cruise, or team sport as an entry point for persons to feel they are wanted and belong before they actually join.
- **Media, drama, and music** offer great places of belonging and assimilation that draw on strengths and skills of newcomers or those interested in church membership.

All these and many other suggestions fit the "come and see" phase of disciple-making modeled by Jesus Himself.[7]

Assimilation Focuses on Relationship-Building, Not Churchmanship

While it is certainly understandable that church leaders want to make good church members of their membership candidates, unfortunately many adults are turned away by such "self-centered and self-serving" motives of the church. Adults want relationships. How can the church offer relationships that matter and help adults experience the church so they might want to join the church?

Building relationships can be accomplished in a variety of ways:

- **Building networks** of persons who live in the same community, who like the same sports, whose children go the same schools, who do not have children, who have preschool children, or who have an empty nest. Get the picture? Networks can be created, nurtured, and blessed as avenues of assimilation and pathways of doing and being church to today's adults.
- **Offering groups** that are designed for nurturing persons and relationships. These groups can deal with personal growth issues, family issues, work and faith issues, caring for aging parents, etc. This begins with academic or information perspectives that might be a next step from the network that is primarily relational in focus.[8]
- **Creating bridge relationships** between the churched and newcomers or potential newcomers. Engage some of your most friendly church members in each of the groups or networks you create so that bridge-building relationships might be formed. Pray

about these persons, and pray for these persons, for their ministry is great in beginning assimilation.

- **Providing personal coaches for newcomers and new members** to create the desired continuity of relationships. The coach opens the opportunity of building a trustworthy relationship between a church member and a newcomer to the faith and thus an introduction to the church family. Personal coaches are concerned about finding the right questions that move persons toward their agenda, and helping them find answers to their search for meaning.[9]

Assimilation Is about Convenience and Relevance, Not Affiliation

Effective assimilation is not about church affiliation or preserving church programs or ministries. Assimilation is about meeting newcomers and potential newcomers where they are, not where we want them to be. We have seen how Jesus modeled this in John 4 with the woman at the well. Assimilation is about learning to open our hearts and programs to the unchurched, dechurched, or those skeptical about church *before* they decide to join. Particularly those from the postmodern culture (persons who didn't grow up in the church culture or in a church culture family) need to feel they belong *before* they will change behaviors or beliefs. That's a real change and challenge for many churches.

What does meeting them where they are rather than where we want them to be mean? What are the implications for the way we think about and engage in assimilation of busy adults? Consider the following possibilities.

Scheduling Is a Real Challenge for Busy Adults

- **"As you go"...schedule**—This means creating gatherings within *their* daily path and convenient with their schedule. Try planning events before or after work, during lunch breaks, or while the children are in their extracurricular classes or sports events. Be careful, however, not to draw adults away from participating in their children's activities.
- **Multiple time frame offerings**—Do not schedule just one time for training. The day of offering training for adults just one time during a given week is likely gone. We must offer it often so they can choose the most convenient time and best grouping for them.
- **One-day seminar or retreat**—This is a more user-friendly way of training today than the traditional five or six one-hour meetings. It also offers better community-building opportunities.

- **Use multimedia**–Multimedia presentations allow the postmoderns to train in the comfort of their homes, offices, or even their cars while they commute.
  Offer a tour of church facilities before or after worship services, sharing something of the history of the church and introducing key leaders for each age group and ministry program. (Treat the guests royally, with a nice meal during the tour).

Resources Are Shifting for Busy Adults

- **Multimedia**–Use multimedia options as the basis of curricula (video, audio, CD ROMs, online learning, Web sites, etc.). Most of today's adults are Web-friendly and technology-savvy people, so we are challenged to use this delivery system for their training and networking.
- **Based on life**–Focus curricula on life experiences and life questions that lead to life-changing Bible study. The best curricula for new members and potential newcomers are their life experiences, not necessarily just printed literature of planned programs.
- **Relational**–Curricula and study options need to be highly relational as opposed to strictly didactic (learner-focused rather than teacher-led).
- **Web sites**– Many sites, including www.serendipityhouse.com, www.lifeway.com, www.helwys.com, www.Nbontheweb.com, and www.transformingsolutions.org, offer helpful curricula resources for individuals and small groups that are supported or driven by multimedia.

Community gathers and programs offered to the community offer opportunities to meet and minister to busy adults. Think about attending or hosting:

- Retreats
- Banquets
- Family gatherings
- Community-based life issue small groups
- Vacation clubs
- Men's and women's groups
- Couples classes/groups
- Online forums/chat rooms
- Recreation experiences
- MOPS–Mothers of Preschoolers
- Play dates for children

- Networking for blended families
- Divorce recovery groups for families

Help busy adults find their gifts and callings, and encourage them to join a ministry team. These activities provide community-building, networking, and a time of commitment for those newcomers and new members who are ready for this next step. The following are excellent resources to use in these ventures.

- *New Beginnings,* by Paul Wilkes, www.nbontheweb.com
- *The BodyLife Journey,* by John Powers, www.lifeway.com

Coaching Questions to Consider

1. On a scale of 1 to 10 (1 least effective; 10 most effective) how would you assess your church's current new member assimilation and training?
2. What two ideas have emerged that you would like to explore with other leaders in your church?
3. What benefits would come from updating your new member ministry?
4. Who are persons just as passionate about this ministry as you are?
5. What are you willing to do? by when?

We move from here to exploring spiritual leadership *as* the church. That is, How can the church manifest itself *as* the people of God in every phase of their daily life and work? How can the people of God become an active community of faith who influence and permeate their culture through their very presence and the activation of their Christian virtues, gifts, and callings?

Resources to Explore

Arnold, Dave. "A Place to Belong: How to Minister to the Hurting People in Our Churches." *Rev Magazine* (July/August 2004): 102–5. Available at www.revmagazine.com.

Bandy, Tom. *Mission Mover: Beyond Education for Church Leadership.* Available at www.cokesbury.com.

Hammett, Edward. "Discipling Busy Adults." *Leading Adults Magazine,* Lifeway (Fall 2004): 30–33.

Hardin, Gary. "Eight Ways to Show You Care." *Leading Adults Magazine,* Lifeway (Fall 2004): 6–9.

Hunter, Kent. *The Jesus Enterprise: Engaging Culture to Reach the Unchurched.* Available at www.cokesbury.com.

McGinnis, Alan Loy. *The Friendship Factor: How to Get Closer to the People You Care For.* Available at www.augsburgbooks.com.

Rainer, Thom. "Reaching the Receptive Unchurched Adult." *Leading Adults Magazine,* Lifeway (Fall 2004): 36–38.

HOW TO GET THERE

Spiritual Leadership
as the Church

9

Reframing Church
Being the Church in a Secular World—
Bridge-building at Its Best

"I'm weary of just going to church meetings; I want to be
part of a church that makes a difference in the world," declares
a faithful but frustrated church leader.

"How can my church move beyond pampering those in the
pews to penetrating the culture for the cause of Christ?" has
become a mantra for the leaders of several churches.

Now we move from leadership *through* the church to spiritual
leadership *as* the church. A great example of this shift can be seen in
the ministry of The Urban Sanctuary in Philadelphia. The people of
God restored a decaying church building and revitalized a community
by learning to mobilize laypersons, build transforming partnerships,
and grow leaders that are committed to impacting communities.[1]

First Baptist Church of Leesburg, Florida, moved from being a
sleepy congregation in a rural small town to being a vibrant and
impacting congregation. They moved beyond their walls and framed

their ministries around the gifting and calling of their membership. Such a venture revitalized lives and transformed their community. Now they have a ministry village with over one hundred ministries staffed primarily by volunteers who touch the hearts and needs of the hurting in their surrounding area. These ministries are fashioned as the congregation learns to build partnerships and alliances with various agencies and businesses in the community.[2]

Church of the Savior in Washington, D.C., has a strong history of building alliances and partnerships with the community to bring the message of hope and healing to a troubled and needy community. Though they've never had more than a hundred members, they have more than one hundred ministries and a several million dollar budget. How does that work? They grow leaders that grow ministries.[3]

Growing spiritual leaders *through* the church is critical and vital for accomplishing the mission of God in the world. The local institutionally based church has worked well for us over the last decades, particularly in the days of the church culture. However, in the twenty-first century, with its realities of a post-Christian world, we are challenged to learn to grow spiritual leaders *as* the church.

This is different from *through* the church. As believers are learning to *be* salt, light, and leaven in the world, they must exert leadership in the world for the nonbelievers. The unchurched are rarely coming to our church meetings. We must learn to "go into all the world" as believers and as the presence of Christ in the boardrooms, school rooms, medical and legal societies, government offices, department stores. Just as Jesus apprenticed the disciples, and they were dependent on His presence before He left them to multiply what they learned, so it is today with the church and the believer.

In this culture the institutional church is losing its influence and often its presence. Now, however, believers are being called to move into their God-called ministries in the world. Through their leadership the good news can penetrate the culture and find those who are spiritual travelers. They can provide a drink for those thirsty to hear of God's love but unable to find their way into the institutional church. This is not to say that the institutional church should die. Quite the contrary! The church must become more biblical so that it embraces the gathered and the scattered church so clearly defined in scripture. Reframing the church for a new century is not an "either/or" but a "both/and" challenge. We need the gathered institutional church to equip, resource, encourage, and serve as a place of worship and edification for those who will come. We need the scattered church that disperses into the world to permeate and to build relationships and trust as God places us where God desires us to be. Then the broken may experience healing, hope, and wholeness as God works in and through each member of the body of Christ. How can the dispersed church be activated and find its presence in the world? What are some bridge-building opportunities to explore or create?

Building Bridges through Partnerships and Alliances That Transform the Community

As the church, leaders must first decide the nature of the church and the changes the church must make to become the church in the world instead of the church in the pew. Eric Swanson has offered much help at this point. He gives us language for this pioneering arena of ministry as we chart the changes the local church must make in its attitudes and practices. I have compiled and summarized many of his learning shifts in the following chart for your review.

Ten Paradigm Shifts Toward Community Transformation[4]

FROM	TO
Building walls	Building bridges
Measuring attendance	Measuring impact
Encouraging the saints to attend the service	Equipping the saints for the works of service
"Serve us"	Service in the world
Duplication of human services and ministries	Partnering with existing services and ministries
Fellowship	Functional unity
Condemning the city	Blessing the city and praying for it
Being a minister in a congregation	Being a minister in a parish
Anecdote and speculation	Valid information
Teacher	Learner

Swanson's article provides some evaluation and planning concepts that assist leaders and churches who want to become more community-minded and community-focused communities of faith. A review of these concepts in leadership meetings and forums provides excellent stimulation for seeds to be planted and for dialogues to be experienced and actions to be planned and conducted.

Charlie, a 78-year-old deacon of an old downtown church, caught this vision. Charlie said he had been serving as a deacon in his church for years and never felt he had made a difference. He wanted his last years of leadership to make an impact. He engaged with these concepts, studied them, and prayed through them carefully. This enabled him in his last five years on this earth to make a serious impact in his congregation. He led them to create a nonprofit, faith-based organization that helped the poorest of the poor in their city and mobilized laypersons as volunteers to help meet the needs of persons in the inner city. Charlie made the shift, and his leadership influenced and provided a model for his congregation to make the shift from being focused on self-service to community service. Charlie's vision and his personal journey not only modeled significant shifts for his church, but the church got on the front page of the city-wide newspaper and on the evening news regularly for the wonderful ministries being done all across the city. The church could not have bought such wonderful publicity. Charlie died a happy man and a man who made a difference. Recipients of his ministry and persons, inside and outside the church walls, shared his impact on them during his funeral service. One man made a difference. He became a respected legitimizer for those of his generation in his church who were skeptical of the change.

Interested in being a person who impacts others, who transforms churches and communities, and who lives a fulfilling life? Keep reading! Begin your journey, and embrace the shifts God is calling you to make.

Where Do We Go from Here?

What does the church need to do in the world? What is happening in the postmodern church of God that evidences that the church is becoming the church in the world?

From Isaiah 65:17–25, Ray Bakke outlines seven characteristics of a healthy community from the heart of God:[5]

- Public celebration and happiness (vv. 18, 19)
- Public health for children and the aged (v. 20)
- Housing for all (v. 21)
- Food for all (v. 22)
- Meaningful work (vv. 22, 23)
- Family support systems (v. 23)
- Absence of violence (v. 25).

This list outlines our potential marching orders. It shows where our world stands in need and where we can join forces with other community organizations to provide help in the name of Christ. It shows us people in need who quite likely face a teachable moment.

Your church needs to look at the list and choose those areas where you have the resources to offer and commitment to stay at work over the long haul.[6]

The Spirit of God is at work. There is a good chance that the next great movement of God will involve putting the church back into community where it can be the leaven, salt, and light God designed the church to be. Operation Inasmuch was birthed in a congregation in Fayetteville, N.C.[7] This focused, strategic plan for building partnerships and alliances between the church, community-based organizations, and public agencies has flourished. Houses have been built through Habitat for Humanity. Multiple repair services have been accomplished through joint efforts of churches and agencies. People have been clothed, fed, and offered medical treatments through these cooperative efforts and partnerships. This is just one approach to building partnerships that produces Kingdom fruit. The challenge for many churches becomes, Do we simply exist to serve us, or to reach the world? Will we join God in this transforming work? For the sake of the gospel, the church and our communities, let's move forward in faith!

Missions Connect is another ministry that is building effective multicultural, multidenominational mission experiences for youth through the country. Mike Hopkins, former local church Christian educator, youth minister and missionary, is the founder. His vision is clear, and his passion is deep. He is determined to help young people experience mission and do theological reflection on their experiences. He does this in a way that builds their faith and impacts their lives as they impact communities across the globe. Impact and transformation are the core values.[8]

Reports from Missions Connect experiences include, "Terri, one of our adults, had planned all year to be a part of the mission trip, but an unexpected medical emergency changed her ability to participate as a 'regular' participant. She volunteered to be a runner and help with video, errands, and whatever. She was somewhat nervous that there wouldn't be anything that she could really do. On the first day of going around to the crews, she met one of the residents, Mr. Tom. They struck up a friendship quickly. He asked if he could have a picture of her. She had someone on the crew take one of both of them and then got that developed. She put it in a frame and presented it to Mr. Tom on the last day. He cried. He told her that no one had ever shown him such kindness and love as he had seen this week. Her talking to him everyday had made him feel like God really loves him. Terri cried, and God smiles."

"A woman who had been to the pilot World Changers project so many years ago heard of a group in need of sleeping bags and mats for the Greer project. She delivered a new sleeping bag and mat along with snacks for each of the students. When another adult heard that she had done that, they asked her, 'Why?' And she said, 'Mari told me there was a need.'...and God smiles."

What Are the Next Steps for You?

- With which paradigms do you readily identify?
- Which principles or illustrations speak to you most strongly?
- How would you answer the question, "Tell me about the impact your church is having on your community?"
- Define your "growth model" for individuals?
- Can those in your church grow significantly apart from service? Why or why not?
- What are some natural ways you can begin building bridges into your community?
  - ~ Where is the "low-hanging fruit" (the most viable and ready ministries) for your church?
  - ~ Where do you sense is your first (or next) entry point into your community?
  - ~ What are the internal/external barriers to entering into the life of your community?
- Which human service agencies would make natural "partner ministries" for your church? (i.e., social services agencies, funeral homes, hospice programs, Red Cross, Habitat for Humanity, Big Sisters and Big Brothers Organization, Salvation Army, etc.)
- What are some ways that you can "bless" your city?
- How can you begin to get good information about your community's "mission field" and "mission force?" (i.e., interview community leaders and persons in your congregation who work and volunteer in community organizations and businesses)
- Consider having a leadership retreat for church leaders to discuss the "10 Paradigm Shifts." Through dialogue, prayer, and exploration of options and open doors, set goals and craft strategies for finding and taking next steps to build community transforming ministries and partnerships.

So how can we build bridges to help churches and leaders live into these challenges Eric Swanson has framed for us? Consider the following suggestions for each of the shifts he suggests.

Bridge-building Experiences That Can Transform Communities[9]

Shifts to Work Toward	Bridge-building Experiences
Building bridges	• Spend more time and money on building bridges than on building buildings. • Put bridge-building on the top of every leadership meeting's agenda. • Create opportunities for dialogue with community leadership. • Create scholarships and learning opportunities for persons in the community who are not members of your church.
Measuring impact	• Collaborate with church and community leaders to determine how to measure impact of church ministries. • Create forums for dialogue about measuring impacts and assessing needs in the community.
Equipping the saints for the works of service	• Survey congregation to determine how and where they serve the community during the week. • Create forums for these various mobilized members to dialogue with each other around affinity areas and their passions. • Seek to discern God in the world.
Service in the world	• Identify needs in the community that others are not addressing. • Identify places where your membership is already serving in the community. Find ways to support, nurture, and equip them for more effective partnerships.
Partnering with existing services and ministries	• Identify potential partnerships that could be developed through your mobilized members already engaged with agencies • Create and seek out creative funding sources for community-transforming partnerships via grants, private funds, etc. • Provide ongoing banquets, affirmation, commissioning, and pastoral care services for community leaders in the profit and not-for-profit world. • Offer care-giving services for community leaders. • Offer hands-on mission opportunities for church members in service community organizations. • Create hands-on mission opportunities, and invite community leaders to join you in the mission venture.

Functional unity	• Focus ministry beyond the church membership to the community. • Design experiences around mission in and with the community rather than just with the membership. • Create a membership venue for community members who share and engage in the mission vision.
Blessing the city and praying for it	• Create consistent opportunities to pray for community leaders and needs. • Create consistent strategic opportunities to affirm, commission, and network community and church leaders around community issues.
Being a minister in a parish	• Establish an office for the clergy in the community and not just in the church. • Offer community transformation newsletters, Web sites, and Web logs for dialogue and interaction for leaders. • Be a visible and involved leader on community boards and in community projects. • Be visible and engaged in caring for political and service leaders.
Valid information	• Verify and validate accurate information rather than nurture speculation about the needy and community needs. • Research to verify the social justice and social service needs. • Create a Web site with vital statistics and narratives about the needs in your community.
Learner	• Create learning forums for leaders and members. • Create opportunities for business leaders, community leaders, and faith leaders to explore wholeness and advocacy issues.

Coaching Questions to Consider

1. After reviewing the previous chart of information and ideas, what are the achievable ideas you want to share with others in your church leadership circle?
2. How could you identify and enlist the help of others who might share this vision and passion?
3. What are the steps to moving your church toward becoming a community-transforming congregation?
4. What are you willing to do and by when?

Eric Swanson's excellent article concludes with a very helpful resource list for those who wish to take this to the next level and do further research on churches and communities who build transforming partnerships. I've updated Swanson's suggested Web sites and resources for your review and further exploration.

A great exercise would be to divide your church leadership base into teams who can explore groupings of the following books, scriptures, and Web sites. The following suggested scriptures and Web sites offer insight, guidance, and inspiration for building a church that transforms the world and makes a difference for the cause of Christ. Then bring what you've learned and experienced back to the leadership group and dialogue about your discoveries. Pray for God's leadership and wisdom as you discern and take next steps to make your congregation more effective in the twenty-first century.

Scriptural Resources for Further Study

Leviticus 19:9, 10; 23:22; 25:8–55
Deuteronomy 15:1–18; 24:17–22; 26:12
Nehemiah 1; 2
Psalms 41:1; 68:5, 6; 72
Proverbs 3:28; 14:31; 19:17
Isaiah 58:1–12; 61:1–6; 65:17–25
Jeremiah 22:16; 29:4–7
Ezekiel 16:49, 50
Micah 6:8
Matthew 4:23; 5:13–16; 13:33; 25:31–46
Luke 10:25–37
John 13:1–17
Acts 4:32–37; 9:36; 10:36–38; 11:27–30
Galatians 6:10
Ephesians 2:8–10; 4:11–13, 28
James 1:27; 2:6, 14–18
1 John 3:14–20
1 Timothy 2:9, 10; 5:9, 10; 6:17–19
2 Timothy 3:16, 17
Titus 2:6, 11–15; 3:4–8
Hebrews 10:24[10]

Web Resources

To learn more about transforming ministries you can go to the following Web sites:

Allen AME–www.allencathedral.org
Bear Valley Church–www.bvchurch.org
Bethel Gospel Assembly–www.bethelgospelassembly.org
Calvary Bible Evangelical Free Church–www.calvaryboulder.org
Church in the City, Denver–www.churchinthecity.org
Church of the Resurrection–www.cor.org
Church of the Chimes–www.cotconline.org
Circle Urban Ministries / Rock Church–www.circleurban.org
Colorado Community Church of Aurora–
    www.coloradocommunity.org/Aurora/aurora_home.htm
Compassion Coalition, Knoxville, Tenn.–
    www.compassioncoalition.org
Creekside Community Church–www.creeksidecovenant.org
CitiReach International–www.citireach.org
Community Church of Joy of Glendale, Ariz.–www.joyonline.org
Concord Baptist Church of Christ–www.concordcity.org
Cornwall Church–www.cornwallchurch.com
Desert Springs Bible Church–www.desertsprings.com
Dream Center–www.dreamcenter.org
Missions Connect–www.misssionsconnect.com
Episcopal Church of the Ascension–www.ascensiondallas.org
Fellowship Bible Church–www.fbclr.com
First AME–www.famechurch.org
First Baptist Church of Richmond–www.fbcrichmond.org
First Baptist Church Winston-Salem, N.C.–www.fbcw-s.org
First Baptist Church of Leesburg–www.fbcleesburg.org
First Presbyterian Church of Orlando–www.fpco.org
Ginghamsburg UMC–www.ginghamsburg.org/ministry/mission
Greenwood Community Church–www.greenwoodcc.com
Harambee–www.harambee.org, www.urbanonramps.org
Hope Presbyterian Church of Memphis–www.hopepres.org
International Renewal Ministries–www.multnomah.edu
King of Glory Lutheran Church–www.kingofglory.com
Lake Avenue Congregational Church–www.lakeave.org
Lawndale Church, Chicago–www.lawndalechurch.org
LifeBridge Christian Church–www.lbcc.org
Mariner's Church–www.marinerschurch.org/lighthouse
Metro Link–www.metro-link.org
Mission America / Lighthouse–www.missionamerica.org
Mission Baptist Church, Locust, N.C.–www.missionchurch.org
Mission Arlington–www.missionarlington.org
Mission Year (Bart Campolo)–www.missionyear.org

Mosaic Church–www.mosaic.org
Newsong Community Church–www.newsong.net
Northland–A Church Distributed–www.northlandcc.net
Northshore Christian Network–www.nscn.org
Northwood Church of the Communities–
    www.northwoodchurch.org
Oak Cliff Bible Fellowship Church–www.ocbfchurch.org
One-by-One Leadership–www.onebyoneleadership.com
Operation Inasmuch–www.operationinasmuch.com
Peace Baptist Church–
    www.geocities.com/peacemusic2001/peace.html
Perimeter Church–www.perimeter.org
Potter's House Christian Fellowship–www.potters-house.org
Potter's House of Dallas–www.tdjakes.org
Ray Bakke, City Voices–www.gospelcom.net/cv/
Rocky Mountain Christian Church–www.rmcc.org
St. John's Downtown UMC–www.stjohnsdowntown.org
The Urban Sanctuary–www.theurbansanctuary.org
The River Community, San Jose, Ca.–www.the-river.org
Turning Point Ministries–www.tpmi.org
Union Bethel AME–www.ubame.org
Vineyard Community Church of Cincinnati–
    www.cincyvineyard.com
Wellspring of Living Water–www.wellspringoflivingwater.org
West Angeles COGIC–www.westa.org
Willow Creek–www.willowcreek.org/community_care.asp
Windsor Village UMC–www.kingdombuilder.com

Book Resources

Bakke, Raymond. *A Biblical Word for an Urban World.* Valley Forge,
    Pa.: Board of International Ministries, American Baptist
    Churches in the U.S.A., 2000.
____. *A Theology as Big as the City.* Downers Grove, Ill.: InterVarsity
    Press, 1997.
Barnett, Matthew. *The Church That Never Sleeps.* Nashville: T. Nelson,
    2000.
Campolo, Tony. *Revolution and Renewal: How Churches Are Saving Our
    Cities.* Louisville: Westminster John Knox Press, 2000.
Cymbala, Jim. *Fresh Wind, Fresh Fire.* Grand Rapids: Zondervan Press,
    1997.
Dawson, John. *Taking Our Cities for God: How to Break Spiritual
    Strongholds.* Lake Mary, Fla.: Creation House, 1989.

Dennison, Jack. *City Reaching: On the Road to Community Transformation.* Pasadena, Calif.: William Carey Library, 1999.

Haggard, Ted, and Jack Hayford, *Loving Your City into the Kingdom: City Reaching Strategies for a 21ˢᵗ Century Revival.* Ventura, Calif.: Regal, 1997.

Kallestad, Walther. *Turn Your Church Inside Out.* Minneapolis: Augsburg Fortress Press, 2001.

Keller, Timothy J. *Ministries of Mercy: The Call of the Jericho Road.* Phillipsburg, N.J.: P&R Publications, 1997.

Lewis, Robert. *The Church of Irresistible Influence.* Grand Rapids: Zondervan, 2001.

Lincoln, C. Eric, and Lawrence H. Mamiya, *The Black Church in the African American Experience.* Durham, N.C.: Duke University Press, 1996.

Linthicum, Robert. *City of God, City of Satan.* Grand Rapids: Zondervan, 1991.

McManus, Erwin Raphael. *An Unstoppable Force.* Loveland, Colo.: Group, 2001.

Perkins, John. *Restoring At-Risk Communities: Doing It Together and Doing It Right.* Grand Rapids: Baker, 1995, 2000.

Roesel, Charles, and Don Atkinson, *Meeting Needs, Sharing Christ.* Nashville: Lifeway, 1995.

Saunders, Stanley P., and Charles L. Campbell, *The Word on the Street: Performing the Scriptures in the Urban Context.* Grand Rapids: Eerdmans, 2000.

Sheldon, Charles M. *In His Steps.* New York: Smithmarks, 1992.

Sherman, Amy. *Restorers of Hope.* Wheaton, Ill.: Crossway Books, 1997.

Sider, Ron, and Phil Olson. *Churches that Make a Difference.* Grand Rapids, Baker Books, 2002.

Sjogren, Steve. *Conspiracy of Kindness.* Ann Arbor, Mich.: Vine Books, 1993.

Stringer, Doug. *Somebody Cares.* Ventura, Calif.: Regal, 2001.

White, Tom. *City-wide Prayer Movements.* Ann Arbor, Mich.: Vine Books, 2001.

Woodson, Robert. *The Triumphs of Joseph: How Today's Community Healers Are Reviving Our Streets and Neighborhoods.* New York: Free Press, 1998.[11]

Reframing spiritual leadership and the church for a secular age is a tough assignment and challenge for most churches and most existing leaders, not to mention our seminaries, divinity schools, judicatories, and denominations. The challenges are so great and the learning curves are so steep that many are paralyzed by just thinking about them. Most are not trying to do anything about it. They simply dream of a "return to the glory days" of the church culture and the European models of education. Well, times have changed and are still changing! Will we sit paralyzed, trying to recapture what was so that we might still be comfortable and feel something of value?

While the classical models of education might still hold value, the coaching model provides relationships, accountability, and venues of learning that can be contextualized and customized to the culture, people groups, learning styles, and needs of the respective leader or congregation. The next chapter will explore reframing leadership training as we look further at why coaching works in today's world.

10

Reframing Leadership Training
Why Coaching Works in Our Culture

Leadership Challenges

"My leaders are crying for training, but they will not come to training meetings? What am I to do?" questions a frustrated church leader.

"My leaders are not committed to the tasks at hand. They are unmotivated and seemingly unconcerned about the church's programming."

"How can I move my leaders from just wanting to talk about things to getting around to doing something that needs to be done?"

Learning to *be* the church in a secular world offers steep learning curves for most leaders and congregations who are from the church culture that is fading away. Such a culture and church was built upon the values based on "ya'll come" to the church building and we can help you. Now, in a post-Christian culture we are being challenged to return to the mandate of Jesus, "Go ye into the world…" This shift brings me to believe deeply that Christian coaching works in our present culture as a means of growing spiritual leaders and being church in the world.

We are now living in a "post" world—postmodern, post-Christian, postdenominational, postinstitution, postclergy. Whether you agree with all of these or not, the reality is that the landscape has shifted. The church is seen by most in our culture as out of touch, irrelevant, isolated, introverted, and out of date.

These many landscape shifts are impacting every major organization, business, and church in North America. Economic hardships have created vast unemployment and reorganization of many—if not most—businesses, denominations, churches, and judicatories. The crises may be just what is needed to bring us all back to reality and relevancy. Very often a financial crisis forces us to examine truths we otherwise might not want to explore or acknowledge. The current spiritual crisis may do the same for the church.

Many leaders and organizations are seeking the right questions and answers to help reinvent leaders, organizations, and structures. Coaching[1] seems to offer the needed companionship, stability, and framework to move leaders and organizations forward. Coaching is about the future, not about the past. Coaching is about well-timed powerful questions. Coaching is about focus amidst overwhelming issues and challenges. Coaching is about a trusted relationship and creating a safe place to grow into new skills, new visions, new passions, and new competencies. Why does coaching work so well in our culture? Why are church, business, judicatory, and denominational leaders seeking out professional coaches instead of consultants or training events?

Crowded Loneliness Creates a Need for Anchors and Meaning

The new culture is experiencing a thirst for consistent, trustworthy relationships. Several elements in our culture are fueling this thirst:

- increased mobility
- a diversity of people groups and belief systems
- a changing family structure
- a deepening spirituality
- a thirst for meaning

Many people are talking about the crowded loneliness in our culture that features many people but few relationships. Companies and coaches are emerging to help people grow forward in marriages, parenting, dating, job-hunting, or you name it. Our society moves so frequently and has been burned so deeply in dysfunctional family systems that people do not seem to reach out to friends. They hire them!

In the past friends helped move you through life stages and grow into new skill sets and relationships. Now friends are too busy, don't have the skills, or are afraid to take the risks needed. Such an atmosphere and other reasons provide fertile soil for coaching. Coaches help move people forward within the context of a trusted, confidential relationship that is not built on co-dependency or dysfunction but rather on questions and a person's individual agenda. This eliminates a fear that "someone, somewhere is trying to manipulate me into something." The time for coaching has come. Do you have a coach? Do you need a coach? How are coaches of value to the church or judicatory?

Coaching and Church Life

Coaching offers a thought partner and relationship for the journey of leadership. Coaching seems to be a natural for those searching, seeking, and wanting to live out of a defined belief system. In fact, coaching may be the rethinking and reframing of discipleship for a postmodern culture. In a rapidly changing culture it may be a path for moving leaders and churches forward around landmines to create new landmarks.

Coaching is a natural leadership venue and support for the gathered and the scattered church. The gathered church typically meets in a building at designated times for worship, edification, and equipping. The scattered church typically is dispersed throughout the week into many different vocations and institutions to make a difference in the world. Both groups need coaches as we face rapid change, growing diversity, and what often seem to be insurmountable challenges of faith and function. Coaching is a great avenue for creating "go structures" for believers who are seeking to *be* salt, light, and leaven in the world.[2] Whether a food coach, leadership coach, parenting coach, marriage coach, education coach, life coach, congregational coach, or organizational coach, coaching can be a "go structure" for ministry and impacting the world.

Coaching offers an opportunity to build relationships–*not around telling* others what the coach believes–but *around asking questions* around the client's personal, spiritual, relational, or leadership agenda. Coaching is perfect for working with postmoderns who want to explore, who intend to rethink, and who are looking for relationships, community, and persons who earn the right to be heard and to speak.

Consider some of the benefits of Christian leadership coaching for you and your congregation.

Benefits of Christian Leadership Coaching

Christian Leadership Coaching

HELPS Christian Leaders to

- achieve more, in less time, with greater life and ministry satisfaction
- get where they want to go, do what they want to do, and achieve what they want to achieve in life and ministry
- achieve their God-inspired best in life and ministry
- grow forward in faith and function with the partnership of a coach
- reach their full kingdom potential in life and ministry

MOVES Leaders and Organizations from Dialogue to Action by

- transitioning Christian leaders and their ministry setting
- accelerating the pace and depth of learning for Christian leaders
- clarifying the spiritual and strategic journey for Christian leaders

ENCOURAGES and Supports Leaders and Organizations Facing Change to

- pursue and perfect excellence in the practice of ministry
- grow in self-management and focus

Coaching—Helps Christian Leaders

Coaching churches, judicatories, and denominations offers companionship for what is often a challenging, overwhelming journey filled with steep learning curves as many seek ways to manage the present while birthing the future. The challenges of transitioning and changing almost demand a trusted coach to be able to sustain the roar of the white rapids and to stay in the boat during the tough days. Consultants don't have answers anymore because cultures, leadership pools, communities, rituals, traditions, and demographics are becoming so varied. A customized approach—a coach approach—is almost essential to help leaders discover and move forward into their vision and agenda as God gives the vision and challenge to them. As an experienced consultant, I can testify that visions should come from God, not from a consultant.

The formal seminary education many clergy and lay leaders have received over the last decades has not adequately equipped them for leading a church in this rapidly changing world. The learning curves are steep, and the challenges are great. Transformed leaders transform churches. Until our leaders can reinvent themselves, they will not be able to reinvent their churches or denominational structures.

A middle-aged pastor I've been coaching for over a year declared recently, "Now that I've learned how to reinvent myself, I feel I can reinvent my church." Coaching was the primary tool he had discovered. He further explained, "Coaching has helped me see clearly amidst the fog of tradition and the intensity of dialogue about emotionally charged issues. Coaching has provided me with the companionship for the journey and encourages me to keep moving when I want to stop."

I recently watched a denominational leader have an "aha experience" (what coaches work for) through coaching. It brought her such excitement because, in her words, it "opened up a whole new dimension to my ministry that I've never seen before." She has since moved forward into new and needed ministry arenas. She declared, "I'd never have seen this without being coached."

I've been serving for some time as a life coach for a group of unchurched spiritual travelers. Coaching skills have provided venues for life-guiding dialogue to those searching hearts and minds. For instance, Randy recently made some significant "life-altering connections" in one of our coaching sessions. He came to understand, "that some old patterns of life are activated when I encounter too much new too fast or when I encounter resentment in relationships and allow it to go unprocessed."

Coaching—Moves Leaders and Organizations to Action

What would happen if churches and judicatories took at least half of the money they spent on consultants and training sessions and invested that in providing coaches for key leaders, key churches, and key groups within the judicatory? I suspect you would likely see more life transformation and reinventing of ministry through this investment. You would discover the potential of multiplying what is learned rather than sticking to a consultant and training model that rarely produces much change. What values might coaching offer?

- *Reframing of ministry descriptions*–learning what to stop doing so you can spend more time doing what is needed to move forward
- *Learning to measure what matters in a new culture*–learning to create new measuring sticks for effectiveness so as not to confuse activity with effectiveness

- *Learning the value of and the skills to build collaborative learning groups and partnerships*–learning to maximize peer learning and build future leaders and systems that have meaning to a new generation
- *Creating a trusted relationship*–enabling growth, spiritual transformation, and life and career change
- *Finding support for transition and change*–helping ensure perseverance, focus, and follow-through
- *Creating accountable relationships*–keeping people and systems moving forward rather than allowing them become stuck
- *Discerning timing, appropriateness, relevancy, and leadership of the Spirit*–learning to take the right actions and make the right decisions in given situations, relationships, and challenges
- *Initiating prayer partnership*–learning to include God in the leadership and growth challenges you face

One of my current coaching clients is a staff group within a denominational structure. This group wanted to learn to think outside the box so they might learn to do their work differently and more effectively in light of cultural shifts and new demographic realities. The coaching experience is beginning to bear some fruit as we discover together new realities, roadblocks (perceived and real), and the strengths and vision of the group. Momentum is beginning to build as the group discovers what is preventing them from taking risks they want and need to take to birth the new. They are learning how to say "no" to things so they can say "yes" to their visions and dreams. The group is beginning to have fun again rather than feel burdened to keep propping up things that really are not fruitful, but are expected by history and tradition.

Coaching—Encourages and Supports Leaders and Organizations Facing Change

Recently, I spoke at a ministers' conference about trends in ministry. A pastor acknowledged to the group, "As a minister I just do not feel equipped or motivated to adjust to these cultural shifts– the learning curve is overwhelming and steep for me. I see the need to make the shifts, but I just don't think I can do it."

I asked his permission to demonstrate how a coach might deal with this stress and desire in his life. He reluctantly agreed. The coaching conversation went something like this:

COACH: Can you restate the issue you want to be coached around today?

PERSON BEING COACHED: I see the realities of the cultural shifts around me, but I feel very ill-equipped to deal with these realities and have no idea that I could face this steep learning curve.

COACH: So you see the new realities and shifts as real—but over-whelming?

PERSON: That is correct.

COACH: What makes these realities overwhelming for you?

PERSON: I realize to be more effective I need more knowledge, experience, and training; but I don't have the time, energy, or money. I do have the desire, but other resources are limited.

COACH: So you want to face the challenge, but you find some limitations in being able to get the training needed to help you feel more prepared?

PERSON: That is correct.

COACH: What could you possibly do to find the time, energy, and money to help you face these learning curves?

PERSON: (*Sat silent about thirty to sixty seconds.*) I might be able to ask my church for some financial assistance.

COACH: That's a great idea! What could you do to help them find the win-win in providing these funds for your continuing education effort?

PERSON: I could share some of the information I learned today that validated much of what I had been thinking concerning cultural shifts in our community. I could share with them that much of the frustration we have all been feeling is due to our not knowing how to help and minister effectively in this changing community. If *I* get help, then I can help *them.* Then we could be more effective in our ministry in our community.

COACH: I can see your eyes clearing and a smile coming to your face. Can you help me understand what you're experiencing?

PERSON: I just realized that I *have* not because I *ask* not. I really think if I share this information with my church they will likely not only give me the needed funds but give me some time to study!

COACH: That's great! What barriers might prevent you from following through on this plan?

PERSON: I might lose the vision and momentum. If I get the time and money approved, then where should I go for training? What's the best plan? (*I could see the frustration and fear rising again in his face.*)

COACH: What would help ease your anxiety and help you find a good plan of education?

PERSON: I think I need a coach!

COACH: How do you see that this would help you?

PERSON: It would help me stay focused and motivated to explore learning opportunities.

COACH: What are you willing to do and by when?

Coaches live for such an experience. In less than ten minutes I watched this "frustrated pastor" shift from despondency to hope and excitement. He had an "aha experience" when he realized he just needed to ask and that a coach was available to help him achieve his desires and goals. Such a demonstration not only created a new client for a coach, but four other pastors came to me afterward and applauded the demonstration. They wanted to know how to sign up and find a coach!!! The proof is in the demonstration and watching another move from frustration to fulfillment in ten minutes.

One Model of Congregational Coaching

As a Christian educator, adjunct seminary professor, and leader of denominational teams, I've been exposed to many, many training experiences, consultant models, and resources through the years. I've certainly benefited from these various resources, models, and tools. I can honestly say to you that the coaching skills I have learned and been the recipient of over the last several years bear more fruit more quickly and more efficiently than anything I've ever known. Coaching offers hope, focus, accountability, and a pathway of leadership development and discipleship that produces quality for a postmodern culture, and guidance for churches struggling to be relevant in a rapidly changing and challenging world.

I'm convinced that some leaders and churches respond best to a consultant model of ministry. I'm equally convinced that large numbers of leaders and churches respond best to the coaching model. Coaching is about action and forward movement in life. It's about connecting the dots of life to make increased meaning and fulfillment. Coaching helps one lead from the heart and not just the head. It unlocks leaders from fears, distractions, bad influences, or beliefs that paralyze them from being all they were created to be.

I would like to propose that churches, denominations, judicatories, and districts begin to cooperate to employ a coach in residence to help grow leaders. In turn these new leaders will transform churches. The retooling and customized leadership development a coach can facilitate will offer support for leaders and organizations during these challenging days of transition. The ongoing relationship with an objective and nonpolitical person can be of extreme help to assist people and organizations move from wandering to walking. Consider the following as a working model ministry description for a coach-in-residence.

Congregational Coach-in-Residence

Ministry Description

A congregational coach-in-residence offers lay and clergy leadership the benefits of a professional and certified coaching relationship that helps ensure personal and professional growth of leaders. Such leadership growth will impact the progressive movement of the church that transforms persons and communities for the cause of Christ.

Benefits of Coach-in-Residence to Congregation and Community

Assists leaders to

- identify gaps between where leaders are and where they want to be
- grow forward in faith and function with the companionship of a coach
- effectively deal with change, conflict, and stressful interpersonal relationships
- move from dialogue to action plans that move them and the congregation forward
- face and deal with personal discomforts as a growing edge of faith formation and leadership growth
- explore options and barriers through guided dialogue, not based on answers or prescriptions, but on well-timed powerful question
- move forward with the consistent support and encouragement of the coach-in-residence
- dialogue with a thought partner
- design congregational strategies and experiences that transform individuals and communities for the cause of Christ

Partnership Options

Option 1: Contract with a certified coach to be onsite during a stated period of time around a major issue, struggle, or learning curve the congregation is facing.

Option 2: Employ a full-time certified[3] coach as a coach for the staff, leaders, and congregation rather than a program promoter or one just responsible for a segment of the ministry. A coach would work from a systemic view, seeking to coach toward action and unity of mission.

Option 3: Employ a certified coach part-time as a coach for the staff and leaders rather than a program promoter or one just responsible for a segment of the ministry.

Option 4: Partner with another agency, network, association, convention, judicatory, or denominational group to contract with a certified coach.

Coaching Questions

- What fruit have you noticed in your ministry?
- What barriers do you encounter that limit your joy, fulfillment, or effectiveness?
- How would the services of a coach provide you and your congregation or organization the confidence and help you need to move forward?
- What is a good next step for you? your organization or church?

Spiritual leadership in a secular age will likely come more through Christian coaches than through church programs or church-based clergy. Coaching is always based on the client's agenda. This provides many unchurched persons security and allows them to open up without fear of judgment or retaliation, and reduces their anxiety. Coaching helps them build trust as they find a safe place to work on their issues in their time as they move toward God and as God continues to work in their lives. Coaching helps them connect the dots of His movement and leads them to biblical truths, biblical study, and growing faith.

Coaching—Discipleship for a Postmodern Culture?

Coaching is not a cure all for all the ails of the church or the culture. I am, however, coming to believe that the skills of a competent coach can make a difference in churches, church leaders, and those spiritual travelers who are seeking God in their own ways. Several experiences enhance and confirm this belief:

1. working with the four disciple-making phases found in the life of Christ
2. exploring the many powerful questions Christ asked during his ministry
3. seeing the impact coaching is having on spiritual travelers

This all makes me wonder if coaching may be the major tool of discipleship in a postmodern world. I've been serving as a life coach for more than a decade, and my experiences through the years suggest that coaching is a skill set and a relationship that God uses to transform lives and organizations. Spiritual leadership will likely find an avenue and channel to others through the profession and the skill set of coaching. Thus I know coaching is a major avenue for discipleship in the postmodern world. I am also asking myself more frequently these days if coaches might be replacing, or at least coming alongside of, Sunday school and Bible study teachers for those spiritual travelers who cannot or will not find their place in the traditional church. The mission of God in the world became real clear for many when Christ posed a coaching question, "Who do people say that I am?" Powerful questions may have similar impact again today. What do you think?

11

Reframing the Journey
Entitlement or Empowerment?

Leadership Challenges

"My church is stuck because some of the leadership refuse to consider any changes that are uncomfortable for them," declared a frustrated pastor.

"Until Mr. B– dies, our church will never be able to make any changes," explained a church leader struggling with clear realities in their church.

"How does a church avoid conflict in dealing with respected, long-time members who are often a barrier to growth and progress?" questioned a faithful and concerned leader.

Spiritual leadership *as* the church involves reframing church, reframing leadership, and reframing the journey. All three shifts take great courage, intentionality, prayer, patience, and faith for most traditional church leaders. Routine has become the norm for many church leaders. It's easier, more comfortable, and more familiar for many of us. Learning to minister in a secular age is unfamiliar, overwhelming, and disconcerting at times. It threatens much of what we have learned to believe and trust through our experiences. Most church leaders these days have an entitlement mentality. This leads them to value a stable system rather than venture out on an empowerment objective.

I just left a consultation with a church where a very familiar issue surfaced once again. It was never voiced, but always obvious in what *was* being said, what was *not* being said, and *how* things were voiced. I've encountered this in church leadership circles for over a decade and believe it is a major issue. "Where does entitlement end and empowerment begin?" Or, to say it another way, "When a culture or relationship has been built on entitlement and its effectiveness begins to fade, how can relationships and a new culture experience empowerment again?"

For instance, I recently met with a leadership team of a traditional church. The church had a prestigious seventy-nine-year history, with most years bringing numerical growth around traditional church programs and a strong pulpiteer. Now the church was faced with ten years of decline. They were facing financial struggles, membership decline, and a large building demanding money and energy for maintenance. Current leaders in the decision-making chairs came from historic families. They had fired one pastor because of the decline; and now they had their great pulpiteer and staff, but decline continued. This is when they called me.

It's almost like a family who faces divorce after many years of struggle and come to a counselor as a last effort. The leaders and congregation were as weary as the couple in trouble. They were expecting a miracle from me. I made it clear I would not come in to help as a "miracle worker" because I am not. I would join them as a coach and see if we could sense God's movement in their midst and move them to a focused action that would lead them to become a fruit-bearing congregation once again. They agreed.

What emerged was the issue of entitlement versus empowerment. The historic leaders wanted to preserve that which their parents had birthed. The leadership group's values were more about keeping what was, rather than birthing what God was leading them to become. They could see the promised land, but their loyalty to their parents and their past would not allow them to go into the land God had promised. They spent most of their time trying to convince me they did not need to change anything. They just wanted to work harder—harder doing all the wrong things that they had already proved would not reach the new generation. Still they wanted to persist.

They did. Now a year or so later they are losing what young couples they had left because the church no longer can minister to their children. Their children wanted to move, and the families did. The leaders' desire to keep what they felt they were entitled to is creating the demise of the congregation. It is even creating the demise of some of those historic families, as their children leave the church that birthed them and return only to bury their aging parents. I received a call from one of the historic leaders this week. After listening to him for over an hour, I gently asked, "Bill, do you want to keep what's good for you, or do you want to be a pioneer and lead the church to its next step that will reach a new generation?" He never answered me.

The Many Faces of Entitlement

Entitlement dominates a church when an individual or a group believes they deserve something simply because of who they are. Entitlement manifests itself in various ways. Let me simply list a few ways I've encountered over the years in my ministry:

- Deacons or elders believe they deserve more recognition or control because of their position.
- Senior adults believe they deserve the right to have things in their church stay the way they prefer because they are the long-standing members of the church.
- Parents with children believe they should get more of the church budget resources and staff time, even when the church demographic is primarily of senior adults.
- Church members, regardless of involvement or financial support of the church, believe they deserve all the care, attention, and services the church can offer.
- Choir members believe they should have the right to sing the type of music they prefer rather that the style that communicates best to those being targeted by the church and those moving into the community.
- An association believes they are entitled to given money because they have always received that money for their projects.
- A staff member believes he or she should always be respected for and protected in the role and functions he or she has always been respected for, even though shifts have occurred in the culture and the needs of the community served.
- Churches believe they deserve the respect of their community because of who they are even when the community shifts from a church culture to a secular culture.

I have observed what very often happens when such entitlement mentality and value begins to dominate an organization or people group. Comfort begins to settle in; stagnancy begins to emerge in leaders and ministries; mission gives way to maintenance values. Often entitlement seems to breed complacency. Just because something seems to be given and appropriate for a particular time in an organization's life doesn't necessarily mean it should continue forever in an ever-changing world. Most humans would certainly like to believe we are entitled because of who are or because of connections we have through blood or traditions. Such beliefs nurture us and validate who we are. Unfortunately, the world continues to change. New community and individual needs emerge. In fact, each new generation creates new preferences. We become accustomed to what once worked. We often feel entitled to those programs, traditions, and systems that once worked. But in a rapidly changing world, what once worked quickly loses its effectiveness. Quite naturally we cling to what is comfortable and familiar. We want to hold tight to what has proven itself among our generation. We must remember, however, that elements of one generation often create a trap for the next. Elements from the previous generation often prove increasingly ineffective in a church seeking to reach a changing world.

When entitlement values become a barrier to living into the Great Commandment and the Great Commission, it seems to me that the people of God must face the divine call. We are to "pick up our cross daily," to "die to self," and to "put our hand to the plow and not turn back" for the sake of the biblical mission of the church. Jesus said that He left us with "power to do greater things than He had done" and was leaving us with His Spirit. He didn't take us out of the changing world. In fact, He left us in the world as His voice, His witness, His presence (Acts 1:8; Jn. 10).

From Entitlement to Empowerment by the Spirit

When the people of God let go of entitlement issues that fuel our personal preferences, our personal agendas, and our comfort, we make room for the Holy Spirit to emerge in our midst anew. Entitlement mentality seems to quench the Spirit and fuel need for control. Empowerment by the Holy Spirit creates an atmosphere for birthing the new.

1. Empowerment releases–Entitlement controls.
2. Empowerment creates–Entitlement kills.
3. Empowerment is about His mission–Entitlement is about our agendas.

Then "you shall receive power" is a promise out of which our future is birthed. "By His Spirit, for His mission, through His people" occurs only among people who are not as concerned about comfort or personal preference, or even preserving the past, as they are about moving into partnership with God to reach future generations. They do not seek to compromise the biblical integrity or the biblical message. They simply want to ensure that new generations can "hear and receive the good news" in ways they can understand and relate to. That is the essence of the incarnation. God came in Jesus—in the flesh—so we might understand and experience.

An inner-city church faced with a decade or more of decline faced a critical decision. They voiced this decision to me on our first call, "Will we continue to please ourselves and do church for us, or will we learn to please the Father and do church for others?" This testimony really summarized their struggle with entitlement or empowerment. Months of struggle and work helped them clarify values and mirror some realities—harsh realities of places their words and their deeds did not match with Scripture. Finally, a breakthrough came. A seventy-eight–year-old saint of the church, trusted and respected by everyone, stood to her feet during a business meeting where decisions were being made regarding installing a new $500,000 pipe organ to appease their preferences in worship. She declared, "Isn't it time we spend some money on reaching others rather than on pacifying ourselves?"

As soon as she asked the question, you could hear a hush in the group. The electricity of the Spirit began to permeate the room. The "aha moment" had come to this group. Her quiet but powerful voice had broken through their denial and introduced them to a faith walk that led to years of flourishing ministry as the laity mobilized in the world and the church to offer the good news to persons unlike them. Not only did this church experience a reframing of their focus and ministry, they recaptured the joy of their salvation, the restoration of the founding purpose, and the experience of "whoosh" as they moved from a compliant church to a creative church.

Coaching Questions to Consider

- How can we build an empowering atmosphere to replace an entitlement mentality among our congregation?
- What are the indicators that our church and leaders are living into an entitlement mentality? into empowerment by the Spirit?
- How can we move from an entitlement value system and mentality to being empowered by the Spirit?

- How is living by entitlement working for you?
- What opportunities might living by empowerment bring to you?
- Who are the leaders/groups that need to work with these and other coaching questions that might help move the church forward in mission and in pleasing the Heavenly Father?

Reframing: Art That Shapes the Future

My grandmother was the world's most efficient "penny-pincher." She loved saving money. She learned throughout her life that she could take something she loved and cherished and through the art of reframing make it new again. Such art allowed her to preserve treasures she loved, but it also made things new and more appealing to those who looked for or wanted something fresh and new.

Church is somewhat like for that for many persons of the next generation. Starbucks® founder has said that a Starbucks® coffee shop is today's front porch. People go to these coffee shops, not necessarily for the coffee, but to talk, reflect, think, meet new people, and fellowship. Such is a reframing in our culture. Computer dating has entered the dating world for those persons who lead busy lives and do not want to go the bars where many find dates. Now there's speed dating. You go to a nice restaurant in town with a pre-selected group of persons seeking to meet people. Around finger foods and drinks of your choice, these people give you six to ten minutes to quickly meet other persons, introduce yourselves, and decide if you want to get to know each other beyond that meeting. If so, the hosts share your information. This is a reframing tool for a new culture. Churches are actually involved in this, too, helping Christians in the dating phase of their lives.

Tom McGehee's *Whoosh: Business in the Fast Lane*[1] is a great book for those organizations and leaders trying to learn the art of reframing. His premise is that too often many organizations establish an atmosphere that generates or demands "compliance." Others, however, generate an atmosphere that calls for "creativity." Creative organizations and leaders know the art of reframing as they reinvent for new generations and cultures. Compliant organizations often cling to the past so much they never ask how they can create to preserve their heritage. The following chart from McGehee's book is a quick overview of some of the key reframing concepts the author suggests.

Coaching Questions to Consider

1. After a careful review of the chart on page 153, how would you assess your leadership style? your organization/church?

Compliance Companies	Creation Companies
Policy-driven	Principle-driven
Rule-based	Relationship-based
Conduct training	Allow for structured and unstructured learning
Forced organization	Self-organizing
Reactive	Proactive
Good of organization over good of the individual	Good of organization through the good of individuals
Measure activity	Measure outcome
Ordered	Chaotic
Closed system	Open system
Patterned	Emergent
Internal focus	External focus
Risk avoidance	Opportunity creation
Confuse models with reality	Understand modeling
Try to recreate past success	Try to create new successes
Methodology-based	Model-based
Expert's mind	Beginner's mind
Tolerate diversity	Thrive on diversity
Seek equilibrium	Seek progress
Deficit-focused	Positive-focused
Create burning platforms	Create compelling opportunities

2. What are the barriers preventing you from being who you want to be?
3. What issues or skills can you work on that will help move you forward as a leader or organization?
4. Which persons could help you with this reframing effort?
5. When can you enlist their help and begin your reframing efforts?

One Step at a Time—Practice Makes Perfect

A valuable lesson for me throughout life is that big tasks and major learning curves can be accomplished one step at a time. You can set your mind to something and decide to improve. Practicing these new truths and skills can lead you to perfection (or as close as we might get). Spiritual leaders and effective congregations in this secular culture are challenged not to *entitlement*, but to find ways to *empowerment.* Empower each stage of the journey. Empower each person's unique place in the movement toward God and to a community of faith. The same is true for spiritual leaders in a secular age. The last chapter will review valuing each step of the journey, not just the final destination.

ENDORSING PROGRESS

Celebrating Each Phase of the Journey

12

Creating Landmarks for the Journey
Religious Rituals for a New Generation

Leadership Challenges

"If God is concerned about all of life, how do I discover Him amidst a brutal and devastating divorce triggered by an affair by my spouse?" was the pressing question for a husband who had just been given legal papers asking for a divorce.

"What can our church do to help the younger generation and the older generation learn from and grow through life events and experiences?"

"What traditions and rituals can we create that might become a meaningful part of a person's spiritual formation as he or she encounters life stages and events?"

Spiritual leadership in a secular age is all about impacting the world you are in with a message of passion and mission. It is also about transformation—bringing the transforming power of truth and Christ to those who hurt, who search, who flounder in hopelessness, and who need an anchor in the storms of life.

The essence of the Christian faith is rooted in spiritual conversion "where all the old things are passed away and all things become new," where the "old man" dies and the "new man" comes to life. Its essence is found in the Easter message and the stunning reality that we cannot experience a resurrection unless we first suffer a crucifixion. Something has to die for something new to be born.

In a church culture, conversion was more often than not encountered, celebrated, and validated inside the church walls through baptism rituals and by extending the hand of Christian fellowship. The conversion was voiced through Bethel programs, altar calls, walking the isle during a service, signing a response form, and/or confession of sin and acknowledging of the Lordship of Christ in a public setting. In a postmodern culture I'm discovering that this conversion process often unfolds through many mini-conversions. These mini-conversions occur over time and across relationships between believers and spiritual travelers. They center on significant rituals and the discovery of landmarks and landmines in one's spiritual journey. Also, the journey of conversion is often more challenging and difficult for many because of the deep roots of the growing secular culture. Such a process and reality has deep and steady roots within the biblical tradition. (See my Web site for passages related to salvation.)

Facing the need for conversion in a postmodern world raises many questions for the church:

1. What does this crucible of conversion look like?
2. How can a church facilitate such an individualized conversion experience amidst the community of faith?
3. What does a crisis of faith look like?
4. How is faith nurtured and shared?
5. What is the role of belonging, of belief, and of behavior in conversion in a postmodern culture?
6. How does being a Christ follower differ in this culture from what it was in the church culture in which most church leaders grew up?
7. What does the Scripture say about the nature of conversion?
8. Are we about declaring a conversion experience, or are we about tracking one's spiritual transformation and life change as one aligns life experiences with biblical truths?

These are critical issues for spiritual leadership in a secular age. How do we build bridges rather than barriers with the postmodern culture when it comes to conversion and life transformation? And how do we build such bridges with the new culture without ignoring or alienating the established church culture? Such are critical questions we will explore.

Conversion in a Church Culture

Conversion is a deep, emotionally charged issue for the Christian church. Churches have various interpretations, histories, traditions, and rituals; but all acknowledge conversion in some form or fashion. While such diversity has a long history in the church, it seems the postmodern culture is calling us to write another chapter in this history. Many from the postmodern generation seem to want and need more acknowledgment of their many mini-conversions as they untangle life's challenges and weave through the landmines confronting them in their culture.

Those from the church culture are satisfied with public acknowledgments of their church affiliation and leadership positions. Serving on committees, being confirmed by the priest or pastor, being baptized in whatever manner their tradition embraces has been sufficient. If the postmodern, the next generation, are looking for more, what does the "more" look like? What are ways we can create experiences and rituals to mark their life events that contribute to their spiritual formation?

Conversion in a Postmodern Culture

The spiritual travelers I have been coaching over the last decade have helped me to revisit biblical teaching about conversion, baptism, altars, prayer, regenerative membership, faith, repentance, sin, and what it means to be a community of faith and experience church together. While I cannot possibly review here all I have learned on this journey (maybe in another book some day), I do want to overview the issues related to conversion and marking the events of spiritual growth.

Postmoderns like to mark significant events. They want to make meaning of life and of life events and experiences. They want to connect their faith and belief system to their daily life rather than live in compartmentalized life, as did many from the church culture.

Let me illustrate. Marti and Ron, a young adult couple, were opening their own business. They had worked hard to find their focus, raise their funding, and create their client base. Now they wanted to commit this new business to God. This 20-something couple wanted their pastor to come and bless their new business. The pastor did not see the need and confessed he did not have the skill set to do such. Perhaps most significantly, such a practice "didn't fit into his theology." This couple came to me because they had heard me discuss this in a seminar setting. I coached them through this. I became convinced that this business was truly a faith venture for them and that they saw it as another step in their spiritual journey. They wanted a way to create a landmark for this significant step.

They agreed to the following ways of tracking and marking this significant event in their lives and their spiritual journey:

- Maintaining a daily journal for the three months prior to opening and six months after the opening, and then sharing that journaling with each other at the end of each month
- Inviting their friends and colleagues to a time of celebration and commitment one day before opening, when prayers, testimonies, stories, and Scriptures would be shared
- Agreeing upon a tangible item that would become a landmark for this experience, that they would revisit frequently to celebrate God's blessings and remember His care and their mission

The landmark became a photo album of those persons who had invested in them through the years. Parents, siblings, professors, teachers, friends, etc., were photographed. Emails were sent with pictures and congratulations and best wishes. They received and sent many notes of gratitude. This became their "Celebrating the Journey" album, which lies on the entrance table of their business and home to remind them of God's blessing through the years.

Now, that is not that difficult. Why could not the pastor or the church have been open to helping this couple and a new business embrace this part of their journey and create meaningful landmarks and memories for this step in the journey? All too often the church culture insists that a person has not experienced transformation and conversion unless they use the church language of Zion or biblical phrases. Postmoderns want to define conversion by the changed life they experience or observe. Language comes out of the experience of conversion. Describing conversion for the person in a secular world has more to do with the change they have experienced than the words others want them to use or parrot to affirm church traditions.

I submit to you that this "business blessing" request was just outside the box of what the church typically considered as a significant religious ritual. I submit to you that the church and their pastor were so focused on traditions inside the church that they failed to create traditions for outside the church.

Discovering Landmarks and Landmines of Spiritual Transformation

The Scriptures are filled with examples in which God calls individuals and groups to build an altar to commemorate an experience or to mark a place or event as significant. Why should we not create such landmarks today? The value of such landmarks today, as then, would be that they would help us to remember. Again, throughout Scripture God is always calling His people to recall–to remember. The ordinances were established to help believers remember. What landmarks could be created today?

On my key ring, I have a key that a mentor gave me years ago as a landmark for a significant event in my Christian journey. I have held that key just about every day of my life since then. Each time I touch the key, I remember the blessing of God and the key to living the abundant life that God has provided. These memories help me unlock gifts and callings in my life that allow me to live into the purpose for which He created me. No one else would know this about that key, unless I told them. The point is that *I* know and that I remember!

Through the years of discipling others and being discipled, I have joined friends, mentors, and people I have discipled in erecting altars to represent various landmarks of the spiritual journey.

- **Rocks** have been given to remind persons of how others see them as a "rock" in tough times. Other rocks represent discovery of a significant life lesson or experience that allows them to build on a new future.
- **Sculptures** have been created and shared to represent God's loving care and how the potter fashions the clay into something of meaning and significance.
- **Canvases** have been painted or sketched to help persons recall and remember significant Scriptures, life lessons, learning experiences, and celebration times.
- **Music** has become significant to many. It stirs emotions and memories and serves to mark a moment in time that is a landmark in the journey of life and faith.

These are just representative ideas. What ideas might you have to earmark a mini-conversion and a next step in the journey?

The flipside of landmarks are landmines. Learning to recognize and navigate around or disarm landmines is a significant phase of the spiritual formation of the postmoderns (and many moderns too). Sin and the temptations or situations that cause stumbling blocks are indicative of landmines. Another might be something or someone that causes us to miss the mark/goal we are working to achieve. What can be lifted up and acknowledged to help persons recognize and navigate around the landmines of life?

No one wants to walk into landmines that can maim or destroy. Persons struggling to move from the ways of the "old man" and learn the ways of the "new man" need help in learning to identify what helps them and what hurts them in making this transition. Spiritual growth involves learning to let go of the old and to embrace the new. What can a community of faith create that helps people learn these skills and follow through on what has been learned? Life stages include landmines and crises of faith. For instance, many adolescents go through times of rebellion, trying to find their independence. Such times often create stress in the parenting role and in the role of the emerging young adult.

How could the church help with these potential landmines?

- Provide mentoring relationships that offer support, encouragement, and a role model for work, life, relationships, faith formation, etc.
- Offer accountability services for those who need someone to ask them the tough questions of life.
- Provide a life coach to those who need a trusted and confidential thought partner and companion for the journey of various phases of life.
- Provide appropriate print and Web resources to help postmoderns navigate the waters of change and challenge in relationships, faith life, sexuality, home life, family life, work life, and community involvement.

Religious Rituals for a New Generation

Spiritual leadership is about reading the times and the people of your age and place. It is about helping find and create sacred space, connecting daily life to eternal truths, and providing avenues for persons to move from bondage to places of liberation and faith. Each aspect of this challenge can easily be tracked in Scripture and throughout church history. A close look surfaces at least one common element of this spiritual journey and leadership. Creating landmarks for the journey is crucial if faith and life are to connect in meaningful and memorable ways. A landmark can be an altar built to help a person or group remember when God intervened or made the divine presence known in a life-transforming manner. What are some landmarks that might be effective altars for a new generation?

Building a Family Album

Bryan, one of my students, informed me one day that he was compelled by his study of family systems to try to locate and reconnect with his biological father who had deserted the family in his early life. I was not even aware that he was disconnected from his father. His search was passionate and often disconcerting. When he finally found his father's brother, he was able to reconnect with him and his family—who just happened to be in ministry also. They were the conduit for reconnecting with his father. What a celebration! What a challenge for all concerned to reconnect physically, much less emotionally and spiritually, after the initial desertion and all the years of being apart. All the questions and emotions to explore brought new spiritual challenges. Building a family album took on new significance—new pictures, new vacation plans, new family night meal conversations, new understandings of family and of Scripture passages. All these became landmarks for Bryan's journey. Our coaching sessions reviewed these to see how he could mark these events as well as do some theological reflection on what this means for his understanding of theological concepts such as love, forgiveness, hope, healing, redemption.

This life stage also intersected with the birth of a second child in Bryan's family and his struggle with his place and call into ministry. Prayers of blessing and dedication were written, voiced, and shared. Journaling about his new child, about what kind of family he wants to create, and about the kind of dad he wants to be for the child became a way of marking the events as significant. Landmarking an event often prevents landmines in the future.

Connie, a spiritual traveler and friend, has encountered some career shifts this past year as she wrestled with various health concerns and the realities of aging parents. All these concerns created some discontent in her nursing career and caused her to open herself up to the possibility of a career move and a physical move. Such brought some anxiety and challenge and moved her to deeper depths in her faith life. During a conversation we were able to identify a landmark that helped her connect her life stage and her faith formation. She decided to make a trip home to reconnect with family, friends, and aging parents. While there, she visited her home church, her beloved pastor, and some friends. These visits reignited fond and nurturing memories. The reconnecting at familiar places and spaces nurtured her faith, reassured her that God has taken care of her so far in life, and convinced her that God would continue being faithful. She was able to reconnect with memories of when God had protected her during other lean times of life and career. She saw that God had eventually moved her to places and opportunities she treasured. She also learned some very hard but challenging lessons. She could ask for help from others, and she really was not self-sufficient. Such memories and opportunities to revisit places, spaces, and people served as landmarks for her and others.

Jeannette, a spiritual traveler friend, called me late one night to inform me that she had just discovered she was pregnant. She was not married, but was engaged. She was struggling deeply with guilt, remorse, and almost paralyzing fear. Jeannette was raised in church. Her parents were in leadership in the church. Though her own church attendance had become sporadic, it was not because she lacked spiritual thirst. She just could not seem to connect with her congregation. Her needs and their preferences did not mesh. The pregnancy was such a shock and embarrassment she did not know what to do.

Because of a trusting friendship we had during school days, she called me, seeking an anchor. Her future husband did not feel they were ready to support a child. She did not want to be a mother, and she was scared. After several long days and nights of prayer and conversation, she called to inform me that there had been a miscarriage. While for some this brought great relief, it also brought great grief to deal with and resolve. How were they and their families to deal with this life shift and faith challenge? None of the persons involved in this life challenge felt comfortable to take their situation to their churches. They talked with their pastors, but the pastors were not really excited about opening up this "can of worms" in the congregation. It seemed to me the involved family members were looking for a landmark to prevent other landmines. The persons involved needed something to mark the trauma, the life lessons, and the faith lessons. We prayed and marked the experiences in the following ways:

- **Books** became a real friend and way to process some grief and to mark the experience. I gave them several book lists and books accompanied by personal notes. We gave personalized books to each other. We then got together in an intentional and safe setting to discuss what they had learned.
- **Prayers** were written in journals, to each other, and even to the miscarried child.

- **Naming** the child became a landmark. The miscarriage was early in the first trimester, so little information was known, and only one doctor visit had been made. Still, they all felt the child needed a name, even though they never knew the sex of the child.
- **Sacred spaces** were created by the families to commemorate the child. We had a funeral service of sorts. We shared grief and launched a raft onto a lake. We attached the name of the child to balloons that were released and floated away into the sky. This sacred place is still a warm and meaningful place for them to visit to this day.

Spiritual Leadership in a Secular Age

Just as Paul and Jesus experienced some shifts in their beliefs and practices when God called them to reach the Gentiles instead of just the Jews, so many spiritual leaders face such shifts today. Most current church leaders, seminary professors, pastors, and other clergy are much more comfortable continuing to focus on perpetuating the traditional church culture than penetrating the present culture with the good news of Christ. This book can be the launching pad for such church leaders to release their grip on traditional ways of entitlement and leap out in faith into the new church in the world.

We have learned many lessons about effective spiritual leadership in a secular age:

- The culture has shifted, and many churches are increasingly ineffective.
- The ineffectiveness of many churches is in direct proportion to the degree to which they are inward focused rather than outward focused.
- The mission of the church today is to find God at work in our culture, not just to combat or condemn the increasing secularization of the culture.
- The strategy of the mission calls for more intentionality as leaders and churches move from wandering to walking in this culture.
- The disciple-making model of Jesus provides great insight and guidance for becoming an effective spiritual leader in a secular age.
- Learning to disciple busy adults is a major challenge for today's and tomorrow's churches.
- Learning to build bridges to the postmodern and the next generation is more important than building barriers, since the

future of the church is about reaching the next generation, not perpetuating traditional churches.

- Christian coaching is a viable discipleship and leadership development tool for this generation and culture.
- Spiritual leadership is more about empowerment than entitlement.
- Creating new religious traditions for a new generation is a significant challenge for spiritual leadership in a secular age.
- God may be moving amidst spiritual leaders in the world as well as in the church.
- Effective spiritual leadership happens *in* the church, *through* the church, and *as* the church in today's culture.

Coaching Questions to Consider

- What are the three most significant things you have learned from this reading experience?
- What are your next steps to integrate these into your spiritual leadership?
- Who are persons that can help you in this adventure?
- When are you willing to begin this growth adventure for yourself and with those who are willing to join you?
- What are you willing to give up so you can embrace becoming a more effective spiritual leader for a secular age?

Spiritual leaders in a secular age are challenged to discover ways to validate each phase of the disciple-making journey for each searcher, seeker, and committed believer. This may be one of our greatest challenges because the church culture focuses most of its measurement on issues relevant to the church culture, and for the most part ignores validating or measuring effectiveness of the scattered church in the world. Let this chapter serve as a beginning point for your dialogue and for framing your own road map for validating, guiding, and discipling persons at each phase of the disciple-making journey.

Finding and Experiencing New Places for Ministry in the World

(Help for Clergy Dissatisfied with the Church but Not with Their Calling)

A fitting conclusion seems to be to ask, "What is next for spiritual leaders? What is God about in this rapidly changing world? Could spiritual leadership be shifting in our increasingly secular age?" The struggles created by a shifting culture are challenging clergy and churches to face changes that are often disconcerting to what they have known in a church-based culture, if not overwhelming. Today we are learning to live and lead in transitioning times. Churches will be centralized and decentralized. Clergy and members will be ministering *in* the church, *through* the church, and *as* the church.

Over the last five years I've encountered an increasing number of clergy persons who are voicing a deepening dissatisfaction with their ministry roles in the traditional church. Some are senior ministers; others are executive pastors; and others are in staff positions with areas of specialization. Because of the perceived trend, I've started tracking my encounters with other clergy as I travel across the country. Four out of every five members of the clergy I have dialogue with express dissatisfaction with their church and/or ministry role. It has become clear that most are only dissatisfied with the institutional church, not their calling. Though not a scientific research project, these observations permit me to share what I have learned through such encounters. I can also recite some of the paths many are exploring and claiming as they find new places for ministry—not in the church, but *as* the church in the world.

Reasons for Dissatisfaction with Local Church Ministry

In interviews with one hundred clergy who had expressed dissatisfaction with local church ministry, three factors surfaced consistently. Below, interviewees express the three factors:

1. "If I don't leave the church I will lose my family." They would then explain that the high expectations of their membership were very unrealistic in that demands to be at every bedside, funeral, wedding, committee meeting, etc., left little time with family.
2. "The church I serve really does not want to go on mission; they are more concerned with maintenance." Those clergy who had grown disillusioned and dissatisfied with local church ministry echoed these stunning sentiments repeatedly.
3. "My training is no longer sufficient or relevant for the demands of ministry in today's rapidly changing world." Many of those interviewed expressed such sentiments as they grieved the deficit of their education, relational skills, and time management skills.

Too often the church culture sets the standard in that the "preacher is the key." Interpreted by many clergy and members, this means that the clergy need to be at every program, worship, and committee session. Such a standard says clergy should understand and champion every project. This has not only created an atmosphere that burns out clergy, but also creates apathy among persons in the pew.

New Emerging Paths for Ministry in the World

As many of the best and brightest clergy become disillusioned and disappointed with ministry in the local church, God seems to be creating places where they can fulfill their calling while ministering in different venues as the church in the world. The drastic economic and integrity issues that have hit corporate America are causing corporations to employ ministers in various capacities to help restore integrity in the business world. Some have been called as the "Corporate Office of Community Conscience"; others become chaplains or pastors in corporate America. The movement of God in and through the marketplace ministry can be tracked more closely at the following Web sites:

- www.avodahinstitute.com
- www.marketplace.org
- www.ministryindailylife.org
- www.workplaceministry.org
- www.transformingsolutions.org

Still other clergy are moving into faith-based nonprofit organizations as executive directors and volunteer coordinators. Brian left his position in a local congregation to become an executive director of Wilkinson Center in Dallas. His ministry has shifted from preserving and maintaining church programs to developing people, caring for the hurting, and serving as an advocate for those in need. He is more fulfilled and probably more effective in carrying out the Great Commission and the Great Commandment in this role than his previous. Many of those leaving the local church are finding their ministry through higher education, consulting, and Christian coaching.[1]

Next Steps for Clergy Who Serve as the Church, Not in a Church

If God is moving some of his clergy from the local church to serve *as* the church in the world, what might be some next steps for these clergy to strengthen their ministry in the mission field? Permit me to list some issues that continue to surface as I dialogue with those I've interviewed and encountered:

- Equipping for ministry in the mission fields of the world
- Networking among the ministers in the mission field
- Finding and using a language indigenous to the world they minister in
- Improving relational skills with unchurched persons
- Learning to create nonthreatening entry points for spiritual travelers in the marketplace
- Practicing consistent theological reflection in such a way as to help spiritual travelers connect the dots of their lives and find meaning around life's landmarks and landmines
- Learning to build bridges between their ministry in the mission field and the local congregation
- Learning to build mission-focused partnerships and alliances among persons and businesses in the community

Next Steps for Churches to Validate Ministry in the World

The role of the church and of clergy is shifting again, as it has done throughout Christian history. Some say we are living out the unfinished reformation. During the days of Martin Luther and the

Reformation, the role of the church and clergy emerged from hierarchy to relevancy among the culture and laypersons. The Word of God was translated into language that the people of God could understand. The ministry was moved from just in the pulpit to the persons in the pew. Now, in an age of increasing spiritual thirst and secularization, we are living in a transitional age. We need both the gathered and the scattered church. We need the centralized church and its programs as well as the decentralized church and all the relationships. We need clergy who lead the gathered church and those clergy who nurture and birth the scattered church. Both are needed, and all will have their own distinctives and needs for equipment, support, and nurture. Such transition demands next steps for the church and denominational groups.

Not only do the clergy have next steps to explore and develop; so do the local church and denominations. What are the steps needed to help resource, validate, commission, and network clergy who are now finding their ministry in the world?

Consider the following ideas:

• The local church can offer commissioning or ordaining services for those clergy who find their ministry in the world.
• Members and denominational agencies need to rethink their policies, procedures, and language to be certain to include those ministering in the world as full-fledged ministers and ministers in good standing.
• Denominational agencies also need to rethink retirement and health care policies and practices for those who find their primary focused ministry in the world.
• Local congregational leaders and pastors need to reach out to clergy based in the world as they design educational, networking, and support-based ministries for those inside the church and those outside the church.
• Local churches need to design validation experiences that provide encouragement and bridge-building between the local congregation and the clergy at work in the world.
• Local churches should design and market resources appropriate for use for ministry in the mission field of the world with persons who are in various phases of their disciple-making

The landscape of our culture has shifted. The shifting culture challenges us to discover what spiritual leadership looks like in a secular age. What is the shape of the church in a secular culture? It seems to me that much of what we have reviewed in this book are indicators of paths in which God is moving His church to be more effective in a post-Christian culture. Different? Yes! Challenging? Certainly! Exciting? Definitely!

Temple or Tabernacle Religion?

Len Hjalmarson published an article entitled, "Toward a Missional Spirituality" at www.next-wave.org that continues to intrigue several of my friends and myself. I do not know him, but this article resonates with me at deep levels and has generated many dialogues among my churched friends, my spiritual traveler friends, and myself. Permit me to share his words and my reflections as a conclusion of this manuscript and an invitation to continue learning and dialoguing. He writes:

My generation was raised with religious life revolving around buildings: a Temple spirituality. Buildings represent settled religion: they are immobile, lending themselves to predictable forms. It was a spirituality of the center, where religious life was influential and expected. It was a spirituality for the familiar places, well-traveled paths, and a way of life that was not strongly in contrast to the dominant culture. It had an established priesthood, mostly well-trained professionals who did the spiritual work for us. The priests dominated the action.

Our own spirituality was primarily personal and inward, and its outward expression was secondary. Temple spirituality was all about forms and gathered expression: it was a liturgical and cultic spirituality. It was a dualistic spirituality: Monday to Saturday was secondary in comparison to Sunday, and the physical world was less real and less important than the spiritual world.

Let's face it…the Temple culture has its own attraction. The Temple is a safe place compared to the road. These are dangerous times, where we leave safe places and become pilgrims. In the Temple we know what to expect. Outside the Temple the roads are not well traveled, and frequently we are off the map.

Priests are for Temples, and Prophets are people of the road. As fixed places of worship become less important, the priestly caste itself is threatened. Priests live in Temples, where they can celebrate the cultic life. When the Temple is no longer at the center, the role of the Priest diminishes in favor of the Prophet. When travelers seek the road, prophets have the advantage: they are already mobile. They tend not to rely on buildings or predictable forms. They are in touch with culture by definition of their mobility. They are already rubbing shoulders with change, and they are friends of transition.

Prophets are comfortable with a degree of insecurity, just as Jesus "had nowhere to lay his head." As the center of authority moves from Jerusalem to Antioch and from Temple to text, from outward forms and places to inward awareness, authority itself is decentralized.

Authority becomes less about position and role, and more about relationship and identity. We move from a narrow definition of priesthood, the Temple definition, to something more universal. We move from places of power to empowerment, from a method to a movement. What was tame and predictable becomes wild and dynamic. Authority moves from earthly spaces to the Throne room above.[2]

Seems that Len and I have been reading the same books and walking on similar journeys. His article summarizes well what I've been trying to point us to throughout this manuscript. Yes, the culture has shifted. And yes, the traditional "temple church" is struggling. But the picture is not bleak at all. Many spiritual travelers are finding and walking on the mission Jesus set before us to carry the good news into the world. Becoming a tabernacle church will be a challenge for most of the current church generation, but for the next generation we will need to become proficient at both—practicing temple spirituality and tabernacle spirituality. The challenge is clear. Who will lead the movements? Who will build the bridges between the movements?

Learning to build bridges instead of barriers with the secular culture we find ourselves in is a paramount challenge of the church and church leaders today. Many want to fight the culture, judge the culture, and condemn the culture and those in it. Jesus walked among the broken, the lame, the sinful, the hurting, and the disenfranchised to offer them hope, healing, and health through the life He lived, the deeds He did, and the hope of God He brought to people and places because of the power of God in him. He seems to be more concerned about impacting those around him than preserving his preferred comfort zone or traditions or practices. He gave up what he preferred when such practices or traditions proved to be barriers in his ministry to others. When he left to return to heaven, Jesus left us behind to follow his example. He promised us he was leaving His Spirit with *us* that *we* might do greater things than he ever did. Do we believe that? Are we willing to learn to live into that promise? Hjalmarson continues:

> A couple of years back someone gave me a copy of Margaret Wheatley's article, "Goodbye Command and Control" from *Leader to Leader* magazine. An insightful look at shifting paradigms, this was just one gem I found there:
>
> *"Whenever we're trying to change a deeply structured belief system, everything in life is called into question—our relationships with loved ones, children, and colleagues; our relationships with authority and major institutions…Those who have led their organizations into new ways of organizing often say that the most important change was what occurred in themselves. Nothing would have changed in their organizations if they hadn't changed…"*
>
> Wheatley helps us understand why it is so HARD to explain why we need change. We can have some ideas about the need for change, and we may think we even understand a new place without being there…but we are deluded.
>
> Looking at the map gives you no real experience of the Grand Canyon. Not until you step outside your normal world or practices into a new world and new practices do you learn new questions, new truths and see things you never saw before. All your senses become engaged, and then even your self-understanding will change.[3]

Just as the ministries of Paul and Jesus encountered various shifts because of the shifts in the culture they served, so it is today. Our challenge is to develop leaders, churches, church leaders, church policies, and practices that will not compromise the Good News, but will ignite and unleash the Good News in a new culture…How many will take the challenge? You will certainly face risks along with many steep learning curves for leaders, judicatories, organizations, and congregations. The challenges and risks are worth it! The world is broken and stands waiting on the hope, healing, health, and wholeness the people of God can offer as we grow into a clearer understanding of how to *be* "in the world but not of it" and how to *be* "salt, light, and leaven in the world" as the church. Remember…Jesus said, "Go ye into *all* the world…"

Leadership and Five Generations

Leadership Issue	Seniors/ Mosaics	Builders	Boomers	Busters	Nexters
Era Born	Before 1928	1929–45	1946–64	1965–83	
Life Paradigm	Manifest Destiny	Be grateful you have a job	You owe me	Relate to me	
Attitude toward Authority	Respect	Endure	Replace	Ignore	
Role of Relationship	Long term	Significant, useful	Limited, caring	Central	
Value System	Traditional	Conservative	Self-based	Changing	
Role of Career	Loyal, responsible	Means for living	Central focus	Irritant	
Schedules	What's up?	Mellow	Frantic	Aimless	
Technology	What's that?	Hope to outlive it	Master it	Enjoy it	
View of Future	Uncertain	Seek to stabilize	Create it!	Hopeless	

Leadership Readiness Inventory for Pursuing Vital Ministry

Review these indicators carefully. Mark all those that you embrace. Then give this to other leaders in your congregation. Ask them to respond also. Then compare and dialogue about your various responses—agreements and disagreements. What have you learned about your readiness as a leader? as a congregation?

Indicators of Readiness for Pastor

- Growing discontent with what is, and a desire to move forward in faith and function
- Willingness to examine carefully your personal leadership style and how you work best with others
- Openness to careful exploration of the effectiveness of your work habits and style
- Openness to evaluate honestly your relational skills with the congregation and community
- Willingness to make changes in attitudes, behaviors, and style to provide new role model for the congregation
- Desire to revisit the essence of your call to ministry and renew your commitment to the biblical mandate for the church

Indicators of Readiness for Staff

- Growing discontent with what is, and a desire to move forward in faith and function
- Willingness to examine carefully your personal leadership style and how you work best with others
- Openness to careful exploration of the effectiveness of your work habits and style
- Openness to evaluate honestly your relational skills with the congregation and community
- Willingness to make changes in attitudes, behaviors, and style in order to provide new role model for the congregation

• Desire to revisit the essence of your call to ministry and renew your commitment to the biblical mandate for the church

Indicators of Readiness for Congregational Leaders

• Growing discontent with what is, and a desire to move forward in faith and function
• Willingness to examine carefully your personal leadership style and how you work best with others
• Openness to careful exploration of the effectiveness of your work habits and style
• Openness to evaluate honestly your relational skills with the congregation and community
• Willingness to make changes in attitudes, behaviors, and style in order to provide new role model for the congregation
• Desire to revisit the essence of your call to ministry and renew your commitment to the biblical mandate for the church
• Intentional decision to support the birthing of the new in your congregation
• Intentional decision to join with pastor and staff in moving the congregation forward in faith and effectiveness

Indicators of Readiness for Congregation

• Growing discontent with what is, and a desire to move forward in faith and function
• Willingness to examine carefully the effectiveness of the congregation
• Openness to careful exploration of the effectiveness of ministries and programming in light of biblical instruction
• Openness to evaluate honestly your relationships with each other and your community, state, and world
• Willingness to make changes in attitudes, behaviors, and style in order to align yourself to God's call for your congregation
• Desire to revisit the essence of your call to ministry and renew your commitment to the biblical mandate for the church
• Desire and commitment to mobilize the entire membership in fulfilling the mission of the church
• Openness to attracting, assimilating, and discipling those from the unchurched population

Engaging in leadership readiness and assessment is only one part of what makes a church effective. How the church sees itself is another vital piece of the puzzle that must be evaluated.

Coaching Questions

1. What insights did you glean from the inventory?
2. What steps can you take to act on new discoveries?
3. Who might join you in seeking further clarity and direction around these issues?
4. When will you take these next steps?

Stages in Your Spiritual Journey

Stage One—Experience Discovery (Come and See)

BASIC DESCRIPTION: Providing entry points that offer the nonbeliever opportunities to express initial interest in, and an introduction to, Christ.

Key Indicators for Assessing Spiritual Journey

- I am questioning life's purpose and/or the meaning of events/ experiences.
- I have a growing awareness of my inadequacy and sinfulness.
- I am seeking a way to connect with a church family and/or those who care about me.
- I have a growing hunger for truth.
- I am curious about friendships with people other than those with whom I currently relate.

Resources to Help You in Your Spiritual Journey

Johnson, Timothy. *Finding God in the Questions.* Downers Grove, Ill.: InterVarsity Press, 2004.
Neighbor, Ralph. *Survival Kit for New Christians.* Nashville: Lifeway.
Setzer, Bob. *Christianity for Beginners.* Atlanta: Cooperative Baptist Fellowship, 2004. Available at www.christianityforbeginners.org
Shelby, Donald. *Forever Beginning: Exploration of the Faith for New Believers.* Nashville: Upper Room Press, 1987.
White, James. *A Search for the Spiritual.* Grand Rapids, Mich.: Baker Books, 1998.

Life Adjustments/Assignments to Consider to Help in Your Spiritual Journey

- Be intentional about seeking out a church and/or a Christian to dialogue with you about your questions and concerns.
- Be intentional about reading the Book of 1 John in the Bible.

Stage Two—Experience Belonging (Come and Follow Me)

BASIC DESCRIPTION: Helping new believers and other new church members connect with the church's theological and historical identity. The connection to their history and heritage is then supported through support structures that have a strong relational dimension.

Key Indicators for Assessing Spiritual Journey for This Phase

- I understand the purpose of the church.
- I am excited about growing in Christ with these people.
- I am finding clarity about what God wants me to do in ministry to and with others.
- I participate in a small group (Sunday school, other church programs and/or support groups) on a regular (three times a month) basis.
- I am feeling that I have a place in this body of believers and desire to fulfill that function (recognition and use of gifts).

Resources to Help You in Your Spiritual Journey

Francis, David. *Spiritual Gifts: A Practical Guide to How God Works Through You.* Nashville: Lifeway, 2003.

McClesky, Dale. *Life Support Resources for Support Groups.* Nashville: Lifeway.

Neighbor, Ralph. *Survival Kit for New Christians.* Nashville: Lifeway.

Stanley, Andy. *Discovering God's Will* DVD. Atlanta: NorthPoint Resources, 2004. Available at www.northpointresources.com

Sullivan, James L. *Your Life and Your Church.* Nashville: Lifeway.

Willis, Avery. *Biblical Basis of Missions.* Nashville: Lifeway.

www.Serendiptyhouse.org–Small Group Resources.

www.ivpchurchlink.com–LifeGuide Bible Studies.

Life Adjustments/Assignments to Consider to Help in Your Spiritual Journey

- Be intentional about exploring the life of your congregation through personal observation, interviews with church leaders, and a new member orientation process.
- Be intentional about participating in a small group on a regular basis.
- Invite an established member or fellow new member to have lunch and dialogue about what God is doing in your respective lives.

Stage Three—Experience Empowerment
(Come and Be with Me)

BASIC DESCRIPTION: Engaging in spiritual life directions through disciplines that enhance the development of an inward journey. This, in turn, prepares one to equip leaders to lead others into a deeper relationship with and commitment to Christ.

Key Indicators for Assessing Spiritual Journey for This Phase

- I am involved in a daily prayer life seeking to find focus and empowerment for my ministry.
- I am involved in a consistent study of Scriptures.
- I am engaged in regular fellowship with other believers seeking to find God at work in our lives.
- I am opening my life to others who can help me achieve the spiritual growth I'm seeking (accountability).
- I am intentional about finding that quiet time with God where I can talk and listen to Him.
- I am seeking to invest my life in the spiritual growth of at least one other person on a regular basis.

Possible Resources to Help You in Your Spiritual Journey

Hunt, T.W., and Catherine Walker. *Disciples Prayer Life*. Nashville: Lifeway.

King, Claude, and Henry Blackaby. *Experiencing God*. Nashville: Lifeway, 2003.

Lee, Thomas. *How to Study Your Bible*. Nashville: Lifeway.

Neighbor, Ralph. *Living Your Christian Values*. Nashville: Lifeway.

Ortberg, John. *The Life You've Always Wanted*. Grand Rapids, Mich.: Zondervan.

_____. *Pursuing Spiritual Transformation Series*. Grand Rapids, Mich.: Zondervan.

Vaughn, Curtis. *MasterDesign Your Calling as a Christian*. Nashville: Lifeway.

Willis, Avery. *MasterLife Series*. Nashville: Lifeway.

Life Adjustments/Assignments to Help You in Your Spiritual Journey

- Enlist a trustworthy fellow believer or personal coach who can help hold you accountable in your spiritual life goals.
- Meet regularly with this person to assess your growth needs.

Stage Four—Experience Mission (Come Abide in Me)

BASIC DESCRIPTION: Engage in spiritual life disciplines that enhance the development of an outward journey and equip leaders who can lead others to align their lives to God's plan that impacts the world for Christ.

Key Indicators for Assessing Spiritual Journey for This Phase

- I am finding guidance, motivation, and encouragement for ministry and daily life through my devotional and prayer life.
- I am discovering I have a growing concern for people/events and/or circumstances around me.
- I sense that God is empowering and calling me to minister in areas of brokenness in my world (home, work, leisure, and/or church).
- I am finding that I'm more concerned with issues/people outside the church walls than about those issues/people inside the church walls.
- I am intentionally seeking to build witnessing/ministering relationships with hurting/lost persons in my daily work, play, etc.
- I am committed to helping fellow Christians hear the needs of the broken in the world.
- I am willing to open myself to fellow Christians who can hold me accountable for being faithful in my ministry.

Resources to Help You in Your Spiritual Journey

Blackaby, Henry. *Fresh Encounter with God.* Nashville: Lifeway.
Hemphill, Ken. *Life Answers Making Sense of Your World.* Nashville: Lifeway.

Resources on Coach Approach to Evangelism

Buford, Bob. *Halftime.* Grand Rapids, Mich.: Zondervan.
Hybels, Bill, and Mark Mittleberg. *Becoming a Contagious Christian.* Grand Rapids, Mich.: Zondervan.

Life Adjustments/Assignments to Help You in Your Spiritual Journey

- Be intentional about doing the ministry you believe God has given you.
- Meet weekly with a spiritual guide/mentor to help you discern and prepare for the ministry opportunities you are finding before you.

Transforming Solutions

These books by Edward Hammett can be ordered online at www.transformingsolutions.org

The Gathered and Scattered Church: Equipping Believers for the 21st Century. A how-to guide to assist in mobilizing laypersons in ministry inside and outside the church walls.

Making the Church Work: Converting the Church for the 21st Century. Coaches leaders and churches to deal with the realities of cultural shifts and their impact on the church.

Reframing Spiritual Formation: Discipleship in an Unchurched Culture. Overviews shifts called for to be more effective in attracting and discipling the churched and the unchurched of a post-modern era.

Also on the Web site are free monthly online deacon ministry and church leader newsletters designed as a resource, networking, and coaching tool for deacons and church leaders.

The following resources can be ordered by mailing a check to: Baptist State Convention of North Carolina, Attn. Jo Ann Walton, P.O. Box 1107, Cary, NC 27512:

Keeping People Over 60 While Reaching People Under 40. (Video and Audio Recordings; Audio CD–$6; Video $15 includes shipping.) Recordings of a popular seminar led by Edward Hammett.

Sermon: "Can Our Kind of Church Save Our Kind of World?" (Audio CD–$6/audiocassette–$6 includes shipping). Updated sermon first preached by Dr. Findley B. Edge, Edward Hammett mentor.

Strengthening Deacons for the 21st Century: Congregational Guidebook. ($6 each includes shipping) A six-week process to assist churches and deacons in clarifying expectations and deciding on models of deacon ministry.

Notes

Chapter 1: Challenges of a New Culture

[1]Ronald Russell, *Can the Church Live Again?* (Macon, Ga.: Smyth and Helwys, 2003). Available at www.missionchurch.org.

[2]Ray Bakke, "Loving the Urban World," *Regeneration* 32 (Summer 2000): 22, available at www.regenerationmagazine.com.

[3]Ibid., 24.

[4]Article by Peg Tyre and Daniel McGinn, *Newsweek* 22 (May 12, 2003): 45.

[5]William Frey, "The New Family" *American Demographics* 19 (Nov. 1999): 32.

[6]Ibid., 33.

[7]Robert and Janette Lauer, *Becoming Family: How to Build a Stepfamily that Really Works* (Minneapolis: Augsburg Press, 1999), 33.

[8]Karen Peterson, "Grandparents: Labor of Love," *USA Today*, 6 August 2001, 1.

[9]Ibid.

[10]Ibid., 2.

[11]Karen Peterson, "Starter Marriages: New Term for Early Divorce," *Greenville News*, 1 February 2002, 8.

[12]Ibid., 9.

[13]Neil Clark Warren, "The Cohabitation Epidemic," *Focus on the Family* 13 (June/July 2003): 10.

[14]Rick Hampson and Karen Peterson, "The State of Our Unions," *USA Today*, 26 Feb. 2004, 1–2A.

[15]Suzanne Fisher, "The Stay at Home Dad," *Marriage Partnership* (Fall 2000): 24–27.

[16]James Dobson, *Bringing Up Boys* (Wheaton, Ill.: Tyndale House, 2001), 54.

[17]Ibid., 133.

[18]Hampson and Peterson, "State of Our Unions."

[19]Wade Clark Roof, *Spiritual Marketplace: Baby Boomers and the Remaking of American Religion* (Princeton: Princeton Univ. Press, 1999), 37–38.

[20]Ross Douthat, "The Christian Future," *Policy Review* 32 (Feb./Mar., 2003): 89–94.

[21]Andy Stanley, *The Next Generation Leaders* (Sisters, Oreg.: Multnomah Press, 2003), 25–27.

[22]Ibid., 29.

Chapter 2: Facing Reality

[1]See www.ssjtutorial.com.

[2]"Keeping People Over 60 While Reaching People Under 40" seminar is available on audio and video CD rom. Visit www.transformingsolutions.org for ordering.

[3]Ron Martoia, "From Gladiator to Irritator," *Rev. Magazine* (November/December, 2003): 68–70.

[4]Ibid., 69.

[5]Ibid., 72.

[6]Ibid., 71.

[7]From Ronald Russell, *Can a Church Live Again?* (Macon, Ga.: Smyth & Helwys, 2004), 2–20.

[8]Prayer attributed to Sir Francis Drake, 1577.

Chapter 3 : When Maintenance Becomes the Mission

[1]George Hunter, *Church for the Unchurched* (Nashville: Abingdon Press, 1996), 22–24; and George Barna, www.barna.org newsletter, May 2004 edition.

[2]I address these issues in greater detail in my book *The Gathered and Scattered Church: Equipping Believers for the 21st Century,* which is available at www.transformingsolutions.org.

[3]Lyle Schaller, *44 Steps Up Off the Plateau* (Nashville: Abingdon Press, 1993), 42–46.

Chapter 4: The Mission

[1]Richard Niebuhr, *Christ and Culture* (New York: Harper and Row, 1951).

[2]J. I. Packer and Carolyn Nystrom. *Never Beyond Hope: How God Touches and Uses Imperfect People* (Downer's Grove, Ill.: InterVarsity Press, 2000), 1–55.

[3]Leonard Sweet, online forum, January, 5, 2004, www.easumbandy.com.

[4]Brian McLaren, "Emerging Values," *Leadership Journal* (Summer 2003): 34–38.

[5]Ibid., 36.

[6]Ethan Watters, *Urban Tribes: A Generation Redefines Friendship, Family and Commitment* (New York: Bloomsbury, 2003).

[7]Robert Putnam, *Better Together: Restoring the American Community* (New York: Simon and Schuster, 2003).

Chapter 5: The Medium

[1]See www.hartsem.edu.

[2]George Hunter, *Church for the Unchurched* (Nashville: Abingdon Press, 1996), 22–24; and George Barna, www.barna.org newsletter, May 2004 edition.

[3]For guidance read Edward Hammett, *The Gathered and Scattered Church: Equipping Believers in the 21st Century,* available at www.transformingsolutions.org.

[4]For discipleship assistance visit a new Web site, www.discipleshipteam.org, to learn about four vital approaches to discipleship and how they might be resourced.

[5]John Stott, *Christian Mission in the Modern World* (Downers Grove, Ill.: InterVarsity Press, 1975), 17–18.

[6]Gene Wilkes, *Paul on Leadership* (Nashville: Lifeway, 2004), 18–20.

[7]See www.pursuingvitalministry.com or www.coachingcongregations.org or www.valwoodcoaching.com .

[8]This involves instructing a core in discernment skills and spiritual formation adventures. See appendix 2 for suggested resources designed to help you discover your calling, giftedness, and ministry.

[9]See Bill Easum's video on "Creating a Permission Giving Church," available at www.easumbandy.com.

Chapter 7: The Message

[1]T-Net International is a disciple-making organization founded by Bill Hull. His partnership with Bob Gilliam continues to provide excellent resourcing, support, and conferencing for churches, denominations, and leaders. More information available at www.tnetwork.com.

Chapter 8: The Mandate

[1]See my Web sites for a listing of coaching services and resources: www.transformingsolutions.org or www.valwoodcoaching.com.

[2]My books *The Gathered and Scattered Church* and *Reframing Spiritual Formation,* as well as www.workplaceministry.org and www.avodahinstitute.org offer guidance for this dimension of ministry. See also www.transformingsolutions.org for more details and info.

[3]I discuss these teams in my book *Reframing Spiritual Formation.*

[4]Barna Update May 4, 2004 www.barna.org.

[5]Portions of this chapter were first published as an article: Edward H. Hammett, "Discipling Busy Adults," *Leading Adults Magazine* (Nashville: Lifeway, Fall 2004): 30–33.

[6]Ibid.

[7]For more details about this phase of disciple-making, see my book *Reframing Spiritual Formation,* at www.transformingsolutions.org.

[8]Many excellent resources are available for these groups through www.serendipityhouse.com, www.lifeway.com, or you can find a more detailed listing on my Web site www.transformingsolutions.org.

[9]See www.coachingcongregations.com, www.valwoodcoaching.com, or www.hollifield.org for more information about coaching services for churches.

Chapter 9: Reframing Church

[1]Find more of their story at www.theurbansanctuary.org

[2]The full story of First Baptist Leesburg can be found in Charles Roesel and Don Atkinson, *Sharing Christ Meeting Needs* (Nashville: Lifeway, 2002). This curriculum piece outlines the ministry of this mission-focused congregation. See also www.fbcleesburg.org.

[3]You can find more of their adventure and ministries by visiting www.seekerschurch.org.

[4]Compiled from Eric Swanson, "10 Paradigm Shifts Toward Community Transformation," available at www.leadnet.org.

[5]As cited by Swanson, in "10 Paradigm Shifts."

[6]Ibid., 4.

[7]See David Crocker, *Operation Inasmuch* (St. Louis: Chalice Press, 2005) and www.operationinasmuch.com.

[8]See www.missionsconnect.com.

[9]Eric Swanson, "10 Paradigm Shifts."

[10]Eric Swanson, *The External Church* (Nashville, Abingdon Press, 2004) provides a great exegesis of these passages if you need additional guidance.

[11]Updates by Hammett to Eric Swanson's list in "10 Paradigm Shifts," 6.

Chapter 10: Reframing Leadership Training

[1]See Jane Creswell and Suzanne Goebel, *Christ-Centered Coaching* (St. Louis: Lake Hickory Resources, forthcoming).

[2]I discuss this in more detail in my book *The Gathered and Scattered Church,* www.transformingsolutions.org.

[3]Many coaching certification processes are available for professional coaches in the business world, and many are emerging for denominations, judicatories, and congregations. Many of these links can be found on my Web site www.transformingsolutions.org. I serve as a coach trainer for Valwood Christian Coach Services and as a mentor coach for On Purpose Ministry (www.onpurposeministry.com). I am a trainer for coaches, a congregational coach, and an internal coach for the Baptist State Convention of North Carolina. (www.bscnc.org). Our certification process for congregational coaches is through the Hollifield Leadership Center (www.hollifield.org) and in partnership with On Purpose Ministry. The congregational coaching model we work from has four tiers or tracks of coaching possibilities. *Readiness for coaching is critical.* We use many inventories and interviews to determine this before coaches are assigned. Congregational learning clusters are also a vital part of this. To review our entire process,

you can visit either www.pursuingvitalministry.org or www.coachingcongregations.org and review coaching for preparing, pursuing, and sustaining congregations.

Chapter 11: Reframing the Journey

[1]Tom McGehee, *Whoosh: Business in the Fast Lane* (Cambridge: Perseus Publishing, 2001), 45.

Conclusion: Finding and Experiencing New Places for Ministy in the World

[1]I discuss the variety of venues in more detail in an earlier article, Edward Hammett, "Alternative Careers for Today's Distressed Clergy," *Rev. Magazine* (July/ August 2003. Available at www.revmagazine.com

[2]Len Hjalmarson, "Toward a Missional Spirituality," August, 2004, at www.next-wave.org

[3]Ibid.